Contents

intelliSoft ventures

EST 2023

Dare to Dream

Disclaimer

The information provided in this content is for educational and/or general informational purposes only. It is not intended to be a substitute for professional advice or guidance. Any reliance you place on this information is strictly at your own risk. We make no representations or warranties of any kind, express or implied, about the completeness, accuracy, reliability, suitability or availability with respect to the content for any purpose. Any action you take based on the information in this content is strictly at your own discretion. We are not liable for any losses or damages in connection with the use of this content. Always seek the advice of a qualified professional for any questions you may have regarding a specific topic.

Introduction To Semantic Search: Concepts And Applications

Understanding Semantic Search: Definition and Key Concepts

Semantic search represents a significant evolution in the field of information retrieval. Unlike traditional search engines that rely heavily on keyword matching, semantic search aims to improve search accuracy by understanding the contextual meaning of terms as they appear in the search query. This approach allows for more relevant results, even when the exact keywords are not present in the text. To fully grasp the importance and application of semantic search, it is essential to explore its definition and key concepts.

At its core, semantic search seeks to understand the intent behind a user's query and the contextual relationships between words. This is achieved through various techniques, including natural language processing (NLP), machine learning, and knowledge graphs. NLP allows the search engine to process and analyze human language in a way that is both meaningful and useful. Machine learning algorithms, on the other hand, enable the system to learn from vast amounts of data and improve its accuracy over time. Knowledge graphs represent complex networks of interconnected information, providing a structured way to understand the relationships between different entities.

One of the primary goals of semantic search is to move beyond simple keyword matching and focus on the meaning behind the words. For instance, if a user searches for "best places to eat in New York," a traditional search engine might return results that contain the exact phrase "best places to eat" and "New York." However, a semantic search engine would understand that the user is looking for highly-rated restaurants in New York City and provide results accordingly, even if the exact keywords are not present in the content.

To achieve this level of understanding, semantic search engines utilize various techniques and technologies. One such technique is named entity recognition (NER), which identifies and classifies key elements in the text, such as names of people, organizations, locations, and dates. NER helps the search engine understand the specific entities mentioned in a query and their relevance to the search results.

Another crucial concept in semantic search is the use of word embeddings. Word embeddings are mathematical representations of words in a multi-dimensional space, where words with similar meanings are located closer together. This allows the search engine to recognize synonyms and related terms, providing more accurate and relevant results. For example, if a user searches for "physician," the search engine can also return results for "doctor" because it understands that these terms are closely related.

Contextual understanding is another key aspect of semantic search. This involves analyzing the surrounding words and phrases to determine the meaning of a particular term. For instance, the word "bank" can refer to a financial institution or the side of a river, depending on the context in which it is used. Semantic search engines use contextual clues to disambiguate such terms and return the most relevant results based on the user's intent.

In addition to understanding individual queries, semantic search also leverages user behavior and preferences to refine search results. By analyzing previous searches, click patterns, and other user interactions, the search engine can personalize results to better match the user's interests and needs. This personalized approach enhances the overall search experience, making it more efficient and satisfying for the user.

The application of semantic search extends beyond web search engines to various domains, including e-commerce, healthcare, and customer support. In e-commerce, semantic search can help users find products that match their specific needs and preferences, even if they use different terms to describe them. In healthcare, semantic search can assist medical professionals in finding relevant research articles, patient records, and treatment guidelines by understanding the context and intent behind their queries. In customer support, semantic search can improve the accuracy of automated responses and help support agents quickly find the information they need to assist customers.

As we move forward, the importance of semantic search will continue to grow, driven by advances in artificial intelligence and the increasing complexity of information retrieval. By understanding the definition and key concepts of semantic search, we can appreciate its potential to transform the way we access and interact with information. This knowledge will also enable us to develop more effective and intelligent search systems that meet the evolving needs of users in various domains.

To sum it up, semantic search represents a paradigm shift in information retrieval, focusing on understanding the meaning and context behind search queries. Through techniques such as natural language processing, machine learning, named entity recognition, and word embeddings, semantic search engines can provide more relevant and accurate results. By leveraging user behavior and preferences, these systems can also deliver personalized search experiences that enhance user satisfaction. As technology continues to advance, the role of semantic search in various applications will become increasingly significant, paving the way for more intelligent and efficient information retrieval systems.

In the early days of the internet, search technologies were relatively simple, focusing primarily on matching exact keywords inside documents. This method, while effective in its time, had significant limitations. Users were often required to input precise terms to retrieve relevant information, leading to frustration and inefficiency. Over the years, as the volume and complexity of online content grew, the need for more sophisticated search mechanisms became apparent. This necessity spurred the evolution of search technologies, transitioning from basic keyword matching to more advanced semantic search techniques.

The initial phase of search technology relied heavily on Boolean logic, where users combined keywords with operators such as "AND," "OR," and "NOT" to refine their queries. This approach allowed for some degree of customization but still required users to have a clear understanding of the exact terms present in the documents they sought. As a result, search engines often returned a plethora of irrelevant results, and users had to sift through numerous documents to find the information they needed.

Recognizing the limitations of Boolean search, developers began exploring more sophisticated methods to enhance search accuracy. One of the early advancements was the introduction of statistical models, such as Term Frequency-Inverse Document Frequency (TF-IDF). This model assessed the importance of a word inside a document relative to its frequency across a collection of documents. By assigning higher weights to less frequent but more significant terms, TF-IDF improved the relevance of search results. However, this approach still relied on exact keyword matches and did not account for the contextual meaning of words.

The next significant leap in search technology came with the advent of natural language processing (NLP). NLP enabled search engines to process and understand human language more effectively, moving beyond mere keyword matching. Techniques such as tokenization, stemming, and lemmatization allowed search engines to break down text into meaningful units, reducing words to their root forms and understanding their grammatical roles. This advancement marked a pivotal shift towards understanding the intent behind user queries.

As NLP techniques evolved, the concept of latent semantic analysis (LSA) emerged. LSA aimed to uncover the underlying relationships between words by analyzing large corpora of text. By identifying patterns and associations, LSA enabled search engines to recognize synonyms and related terms, thereby improving the relevance of search results. This approach represented a significant step towards semantic understanding, but it still had limitations in capturing complex contextual nuances.

The introduction of machine learning further revolutionized search technologies. Machine learning algorithms allowed search engines to learn from vast amounts of data and continuously improve their accuracy over time. One notable development was the use of vector space models, where words and documents were represented as vectors in a multi-dimensional space. This representation enabled search engines to measure the similarity between words and documents, facilitating more accurate matching based on meaning rather than exact phrasing.

Concurrently, the development of knowledge graphs brought another layer of sophistication to search technologies. Knowledge graphs represented information as interconnected nodes and edges, capturing the relationships between entities. This structured representation allowed search engines to understand the context and relevance of entities inside a query. For example, a search for "capital of France" would not only match documents containing the exact phrase but also recognize that "Paris" is the relevant entity. Knowledge graphs significantly enhanced the ability of search engines to provide precise and contextually relevant results.

The convergence of NLP, machine learning, and knowledge graphs laid the foundation for modern semantic search. Semantic search engines aim to understand the meaning behind user queries and deliver results that align with the user's intent, even if the exact keywords are not present. This approach addresses the limitations of traditional keyword-based search and provides a more intuitive and efficient search experience.

One of the key techniques employed in semantic search is named entity recognition (NER). NER identifies and classifies entities inside text, such as names of people, places, and organizations. By recognizing these entities, search engines can better understand the context of a query and retrieve relevant information. For instance, a search for "CEO of Apple" would recognize "Apple" as a company and "CEO" as a role, returning results related to the current CEO of Apple Inc.

Another crucial technique in semantic search is the use of word embeddings. Word embeddings are vector representations of words in a continuous vector space, where words with similar meanings are located closer together. This representation allows search engines to recognize synonyms and related terms, providing more accurate and contextually relevant results. For example, a search for "automobile" would also return results for "car" because the word embeddings capture the semantic similarity between these terms.

Contextual understanding is a cornerstone of semantic search. By analyzing the surrounding words and phrases, search engines can disambiguate terms with multiple meanings and provide results that align with the user's intent. For example, the word "Java" could refer to a programming language, an island in Indonesia, or a type of coffee. Semantic search engines use contextual clues to determine the intended meaning and deliver the most relevant results.

User behavior and preferences also play a significant role in semantic search. By analyzing users' search history, click patterns, and other interactions, search engines can personalize results to better match individual preferences. This personalization enhances the search experience, making it more efficient and satisfying for users. For instance, a user who frequently searches for technology-related topics may receive more relevant results for a query like "latest innovations."

The evolution from keyword-based search to semantic search represents a paradigm shift in information retrieval. Traditional keyword matching was limited by its reliance on exact terms, often leading to irrelevant results. Semantic search, on the other hand, focuses on understanding the meaning and context behind user queries, delivering more accurate and relevant results. This shift has been driven by advancements in NLP, machine learning, and knowledge representation, enabling search engines to process and understand human language more effectively.

As we look to the future, the importance of semantic search will continue to grow. With the increasing complexity of information and the proliferation of online content, users will demand more intuitive and efficient search experiences. Advances in artificial intelligence and machine learning will further enhance the capabilities of semantic search engines, enabling them to understand and respond to user queries with even greater accuracy and contextual awareness.

In conclusion, the journey from keyword-based search to semantic search has been marked by significant advancements in technology and methodology. From the early days of Boolean logic to the sophisticated techniques of NLP, machine learning, and knowledge graphs, search technologies have evolved to better understand and meet the needs of users. Semantic search represents the culmination of these advancements, providing a more intuitive, accurate, and contextually relevant search experience. As technology continues to evolve, the future of search will undoubtedly be shaped by the ongoing quest to understand and fulfill the intent behind every user query.

Understanding how semantic search operates requires delving into the algorithms and techniques that power it. Semantic search aims to comprehend the intent and contextual meaning behind user queries, delivering more precise and relevant results. This section explores the fundamental algorithms and techniques that enable semantic search to achieve its objectives.

One of the foundational techniques in semantic search is the use of natural language understanding (NLU). NLU involves parsing and interpreting human language in a manner that machines can comprehend. This process includes breaking down sentences into their constituent parts, such as nouns, verbs, and adjectives, and understanding their grammatical roles. By doing so, search engines can grasp the structure and meaning of a query, rather than just matching keywords.

Another critical component of semantic search is the implementation of machine learning models. These models are trained on vast datasets to recognize patterns and relationships inside the data. For instance, supervised learning algorithms can be used to classify and rank search results based on their relevance to the query. By learning from previous searches and user interactions, these models continuously improve their accuracy and effectiveness.

Deep learning, a subset of machine learning, has also significantly contributed to the advancement of semantic search. Techniques such as convolutional neural networks (CNNs) and recurrent neural networks (RNNs) enable search engines to process and understand complex language patterns and contextual nuances. These neural networks are designed to mimic the human brain's structure and function, allowing them to recognize intricate relationships between words and phrases.

One of the most important techniques in semantic search is the use of vector space models. In these models, words and documents are represented as vectors in a multi-dimensional space. The proximity between vectors indicates the similarity between the words or documents they represent. For example, words with similar meanings, such as "happy" and "joyful," will be located closer together in the vector space. This representation allows search engines to understand synonyms and related terms, providing more accurate and contextually relevant results.

Named entity recognition (NER) is another essential technique employed in semantic search. NER involves identifying and classifying entities inside a text, such as names of people, places, organizations, and dates. By recognizing these entities, search engines can better understand the context and relevance of a query. For instance, if a user searches for "president of the United States," the search engine can identify "president" as a role and "United States" as a location, returning results related to the current president.

In addition to NER, semantic search also relies on disambiguation techniques. Disambiguation involves resolving the ambiguity of words or phrases that have multiple meanings. For example, the word "apple" could refer to the fruit or the technology company. By analyzing the context in which the word is used, search engines can determine the intended meaning and provide appropriate results. This is achieved through techniques such as context analysis and co-occurrence analysis, which examine the surrounding words and phrases to infer the correct meaning.

Another vital aspect of semantic search is the use of knowledge bases. Knowledge bases are structured repositories of information that store facts and relationships between entities. By leveraging these repositories, search engines can access a wealth of contextual knowledge that enhances their understanding of queries. For example, a knowledge base might store information about famous landmarks, historical events, and notable figures, allowing the search engine to provide more accurate and contextually relevant results.

Personalization is also a key technique in semantic search. By analyzing user behavior, preferences, and search history, search engines can tailor results to better match individual needs and interests. This personalization ensures that users receive results that are not only relevant to their queries but also aligned with their unique preferences. For instance, a user who frequently searches for sports-related topics might receive more sports-related results for a query like "latest news."

The integration of these techniques allows semantic search to move beyond simple keyword matching and deliver more meaningful and relevant results. By understanding the intent and context behind user queries, semantic search engines can provide a more intuitive and efficient search experience. As technology continues to evolve, the algorithms and techniques that power semantic search will undoubtedly become more sophisticated, further enhancing their ability to meet the needs of users.

In the end, semantic search represents a significant advancement in the field of information retrieval. By leveraging natural language understanding, machine learning, deep learning, vector space models, named entity recognition, disambiguation, knowledge bases, and personalization, semantic search engines can comprehend the intent and context behind user queries. This enables them to deliver more precise and relevant results, providing a more intuitive and efficient search experience. As we continue to explore and refine these algorithms and techniques, the potential for semantic search to transform the way we access and interact with information is immense.

Semantic search has emerged as a transformative technology that is reshaping the way various industries access and utilize information. By understanding the context and intent behind user queries, semantic search engines can provide highly relevant and accurate results, thereby enhancing decision-making processes, improving customer experiences, and driving operational efficiencies. This section explores the diverse applications of semantic search across multiple industries, highlighting its impact and potential.

In the finance sector, semantic search is revolutionizing the way financial institutions analyze and interpret vast amounts of data. Traditional data retrieval methods often fall short in capturing the nuanced relationships between financial terms and concepts. Semantic search, however, can understand the context of financial queries, enabling more precise and insightful analysis. For instance, investment firms can use semantic search to identify emerging market trends by analyzing news articles, financial reports, and social media posts. By understanding the sentiment and context behind these sources, firms can make more informed investment decisions. Additionally, semantic search can enhance risk management by identifying potential threats and opportunities hidden inside unstructured data, such as regulatory documents and market analyses.

The healthcare industry is another domain where semantic search is making significant strides. Medical professionals often face the challenge of sifting through extensive volumes of research papers, clinical trials, and patient records to find relevant information. Semantic search can streamline this process by understanding the medical terminology and context inside these documents. For example, a doctor searching for treatment options for a rare disease can use semantic search to find relevant clinical trials, research studies, and patient case reports, even if the exact keywords are not present. This capability not only saves time but also ensures that healthcare providers have access to the most up-to-date and pertinent information, ultimately improving patient care.

In the legal field, semantic search is transforming how lawyers and legal researchers access and interpret legal documents. Traditional keyword-based search methods often yield an overwhelming number of irrelevant results, making it difficult to find the most pertinent information. Semantic search, on the other hand, can understand the legal context and relationships between terms, providing more accurate and relevant results. For instance, a lawyer researching case law for a specific legal issue can use semantic search to find cases with similar fact patterns and legal arguments, even if the exact terms differ. This capability enhances the efficiency and effectiveness of legal research, allowing lawyers to build stronger cases and make more informed legal decisions.

The e-commerce industry is leveraging semantic search to improve the shopping experience for consumers. Traditional search engines often struggle to understand the intent behind vague or ambiguous product queries, leading to irrelevant search results. Semantic search addresses this challenge by comprehending the context and meaning behind consumer queries. For instance, if a shopper searches for "summer shoes for hiking," a semantic search engine can understand the intent and provide relevant product recommendations, even if the exact phrase does not appear in product descriptions. This capability enhances the shopping experience by delivering more accurate and personalized results, increasing customer satisfaction and driving sales.

In the field of education, semantic search is transforming how students and educators access and utilize academic resources. Traditional search methods often yield an overwhelming number of irrelevant results, making it difficult to find the most pertinent information. Semantic search, however, can understand the educational context and relationships between terms, providing more accurate and relevant results. For example, a student researching a specific topic for a paper can use semantic search to find relevant academic articles, textbooks, and lecture notes, even if the exact keywords differ. This capability enhances the efficiency and effectiveness of academic research, allowing students to access the most relevant information and improve their learning outcomes.

The customer support industry is also benefiting from the capabilities of semantic search. Traditional keyword-based search methods often yield an overwhelming number of irrelevant results, making it difficult for support agents to find the most pertinent information. Semantic search, on the other hand, can understand the context and relationships between terms, providing more accurate and relevant results. For instance, a support agent searching for a solution to a specific customer issue can use semantic search to find relevant knowledge base articles, troubleshooting guides, and customer case studies, even if the exact terms differ. This capability enhances the efficiency and effectiveness of customer support, allowing agents to resolve issues more quickly and improve customer satisfaction.

In the realm of human resources, semantic search is enhancing the recruitment process by improving the matching of job candidates with job openings. Traditional keyword-based search methods often struggle to capture the nuanced relationships between job descriptions and candidate resumes, leading to less-than-optimal matches. Semantic search, however, can understand the context and meaning behind job descriptions and resumes, providing more accurate and relevant matches. For example, a recruiter searching for candidates with experience in "project management" can use semantic search to find candidates with relevant skills and experience, even if the exact term does not appear in their resumes. This capability enhances the efficiency and effectiveness of the recruitment process, allowing recruiters to find the best candidates for job openings.

To sum it up, semantic search is having a profound impact across various industries by enhancing the accuracy and relevance of information retrieval. By understanding the context and intent behind user queries, semantic search engines are enabling more informed decision-making, improving customer experiences, and driving operational efficiencies. As technology continues to evolve, the applications of semantic search will undoubtedly expand, further transforming the way industries access and utilize information.

Advantages and Challenges of Implementing Semantic Search

Semantic search represents a significant leap forward in the field of information retrieval, offering numerous benefits over traditional keyword-based search methods. However, its implementation is not without challenges. This section explores the various advantages and challenges associated with implementing semantic search, providing a comprehensive understanding of its potential and limitations.

One of the primary advantages of semantic search is its ability to deliver more accurate and relevant search results. Unlike traditional search methods that rely on exact keyword matches, semantic search understands the context and meaning behind user queries. This context-aware approach enables search engines to retrieve information that is more closely aligned with the user's intent, even if the exact keywords are not present in the documents. For instance, a user searching for "weather forecast for tomorrow" can receive results that include phrases like "tomorrow's weather prediction" or "next day's weather outlook," enhancing the overall search experience.

Another significant advantage of semantic search is its capacity to handle natural language queries. Users often phrase their searches in conversational language, and semantic search engines are designed to interpret and respond to these queries effectively. This natural language processing capability makes search interactions more intuitive and user-friendly, reducing the need for users to formulate precise keyword-based queries. As a result, users can engage with search engines in a more natural and convenient manner, leading to increased satisfaction and efficiency.

Semantic search also excels in understanding and disambiguating polysemous words—words with multiple meanings. Traditional search engines may struggle to determine the intended meaning of such words, leading to irrelevant results. Semantic search, however, leverages contextual clues to discern the correct interpretation of polysemous terms. For example, the word "bank" can refer to a financial institution, the side of a river, or a place to store something. By analyzing the surrounding context, semantic search can accurately identify the user's intended meaning and provide appropriate results.

Furthermore, semantic search enhances the discoverability of information by recognizing synonyms and related terms. This synonym recognition capability ensures that users receive comprehensive results, even if they use different words to describe the same concept. For example, a search for "automobile repair" can yield results related to "car maintenance" or "vehicle servicing," offering a broader and more inclusive set of information. This ability to bridge lexical gaps is particularly valuable in domains where terminology can vary widely, such as healthcare, legal research, and academic studies.

Despite these advantages, implementing semantic search comes with its own set of challenges. One of the foremost challenges is the complexity of developing and maintaining the underlying algorithms and models. Semantic search relies on sophisticated techniques such as natural language processing, machine learning, and entity recognition, which require substantial computational resources and expertise. Building and fine-tuning these models to achieve high accuracy and relevance demands significant time, effort, and specialized knowledge.

Another challenge is the need for extensive and high-quality training data. Machine learning models used in semantic search must be trained on large datasets to recognize patterns and relationships effectively. Acquiring and curating such datasets can be a daunting task, especially in specialized domains where labeled data may be scarce. Additionally, ensuring the quality and diversity of training data is crucial to prevent biases and ensure that the search engine performs well across different contexts and user queries.

The dynamic and evolving nature of language also poses a challenge for semantic search. Language is constantly changing, with new words, phrases, and meanings emerging over time. Semantic search engines must continuously adapt to these linguistic shifts to remain relevant and effective. This requires ongoing updates and retraining of models, which can be resource-intensive and challenging to manage.

Privacy and security concerns are another important consideration when implementing semantic search. The processing and analysis of user queries involve handling sensitive and personal information, raising potential privacy issues. Ensuring that user data is protected and used responsibly is paramount to maintaining user trust and complying with regulatory requirements. Implementing robust data anonymization, encryption, and access control measures is essential to safeguard user privacy and security.

Additionally, the interpretability and transparency of semantic search models can be a challenge. Machine learning and deep learning models, which are often used in semantic search, can be complex and difficult to interpret. Understanding how these models arrive at specific search results is important for debugging, improving performance, and addressing potential biases. Developing techniques to enhance the interpretability and explainability of semantic search models is an ongoing area of research and development.

Another challenge is integrating semantic search with existing systems and workflows. Organizations may already have established search infrastructures and processes that rely on traditional keyword-based methods. Transitioning to semantic search requires careful planning, integration, and potential reconfiguration of existing systems. This integration process can be complex and may require collaboration between different teams and stakeholders to ensure a seamless transition.

Lastly, the performance and scalability of semantic search engines are critical considerations. Semantic search algorithms can be computationally intensive, requiring significant processing power and memory. Ensuring that the search engine can handle large volumes of queries efficiently and provide real-time responses is essential for delivering a satisfactory user experience. Optimizing the performance and scalability of semantic search systems is an ongoing challenge that requires continuous monitoring and improvement.

Conclusively, semantic search offers numerous advantages, including more accurate and relevant search results, the ability to handle natural language queries, disambiguation of polysemous words, and recognition of synonyms and related terms. These benefits enhance the overall search experience, making it more intuitive, user-friendly, and comprehensive. However, implementing semantic search also presents several challenges, such as the complexity of developing and maintaining algorithms, the need for extensive training data, the dynamic nature of language, privacy and security concerns, interpretability issues, integration with existing systems, and performance and scalability considerations. Addressing these challenges requires ongoing research, development, and collaboration to fully realize the potential of semantic search and harness its transformative capabilities.

In recent years, semantic search has emerged as a transformative technology, offering enhanced information retrieval capabilities across various sectors. This section will delve into several case studies that highlight the successful implementation of semantic search in different industries. These case studies will illustrate the versatility and effectiveness of semantic search in addressing unique challenges and improving operational efficiencies.

One notable case study involves a global retail giant that sought to improve its online shopping experience. The company faced challenges with its traditional search engine, which often returned irrelevant results due to its reliance on keyword matching. To address this, the retailer implemented a semantic search engine capable of understanding the context and intent behind customer queries. By leveraging advanced natural language processing techniques, the new search engine could interpret complex queries and provide more accurate and relevant product recommendations. For example, a search for "eco-friendly kitchen appliances" would yield a curated list of products meeting specific environmental criteria, even if the exact phrase did not appear in product descriptions. This implementation led to a significant increase in customer satisfaction and a notable boost in sales.

Another compelling example is found in the pharmaceutical industry, where a leading research organization aimed to streamline its drug discovery process. The organization dealt with vast amounts of scientific literature, clinical trial data, and research reports. Traditional search methods were inadequate for navigating this extensive information landscape. By adopting a semantic search solution, the organization enabled researchers to find relevant studies and data more efficiently. The search engine's ability to understand scientific terminology and context allowed researchers to uncover critical insights and connections that might have been overlooked. This enhancement not only accelerated the drug discovery process but also improved the overall quality of research outcomes.

In the media and entertainment sector, a major streaming service provider faced the challenge of helping users discover content that matched their preferences. The traditional search system often failed to capture the nuances of user interests, leading to suboptimal recommendations. By integrating a semantic search engine, the provider could analyze user behavior, preferences, and viewing history to deliver personalized content suggestions. For instance, a user interested in "historical dramas with strong female leads" would receive tailored recommendations that closely aligned with their interests. This implementation resulted in increased user engagement and retention, as viewers were more likely to find content that resonated with them.

The financial services industry also offers a noteworthy case study. A prominent investment firm sought to enhance its market analysis capabilities by leveraging semantic search. The firm needed to analyze vast amounts of unstructured data, including news articles, financial reports, and social media posts, to identify emerging trends and investment opportunities. By deploying a semantic search engine, the firm could interpret the sentiment and context of various data sources, providing more accurate and actionable insights. For example, the search engine could identify potential market shifts by analyzing the tone and content of news articles related to specific industries. This capability enabled the firm to make more informed investment decisions and stay ahead of market trends.

In the field of education, a renowned university library implemented semantic search to improve access to academic resources. The library housed an extensive collection of books, journals, and research papers, making it challenging for students and faculty to find relevant materials. Traditional keyword-based search methods often yielded an overwhelming number of results, many of which were not pertinent to the user's query. By adopting a semantic search engine, the library could provide more precise and contextually relevant search results. For instance, a search for "sustainable urban development" would return a curated list of academic papers and books directly related to the topic, even if the exact keywords varied. This implementation significantly enhanced the research experience for students and faculty, allowing them to access the most relevant resources more efficiently.

In the healthcare sector, a leading hospital network utilized semantic search to improve patient care and clinical decision-making. The network faced the challenge of managing and accessing vast amounts of patient data, medical records, and research findings. Traditional search methods were often inadequate for retrieving contextually relevant information. By implementing a semantic search engine, the hospital network could better understand medical terminology and context, enabling healthcare providers to find pertinent information more quickly. For example, a search for "treatment options for type 2 diabetes in elderly patients" would yield a comprehensive list of relevant clinical guidelines, research studies, and patient case reports. This capability improved the quality of patient care by ensuring that healthcare providers had access to the most up-to-date and relevant information.

Another interesting case study comes from the legal industry, where a prominent law firm sought to enhance its legal research capabilities. The firm dealt with an extensive repository of legal documents, case law, and regulatory texts. Traditional search methods often resulted in an overwhelming number of irrelevant results, making it difficult for lawyers to find the most pertinent information. By adopting a semantic search engine, the firm could provide more accurate and contextually relevant search results. For example, a search for "intellectual property disputes in the technology sector" would return a curated list of relevant cases, legal opinions, and regulatory texts. This implementation improved the efficiency and effectiveness of legal research, allowing lawyers to build stronger cases and make more informed legal decisions.

In the end, these case studies demonstrate the transformative potential of semantic search across various industries. By understanding the context and intent behind user queries, semantic search engines can provide more accurate and relevant results, leading to improved operational efficiencies, enhanced decision-making, and increased user satisfaction. As technology continues to evolve, the applications of semantic search will undoubtedly expand, further revolutionizing the way organizations access and utilize information.

As we look towards the horizon, the landscape of semantic search is poised for remarkable advancements. The ongoing evolution in related technologies promises to bring forth innovations that will further enhance the capabilities of semantic search engines. This section delves into anticipated trends and pioneering developments that are likely to shape the future of semantic search, providing a glimpse into what lies ahead for this transformative technology.

One of the most significant trends expected to influence semantic search is the integration of artificial intelligence (AI) and machine learning (ML) at even deeper levels. While these technologies already play a crucial role in current semantic search systems, their future iterations are likely to exhibit even greater sophistication. Advanced AI and ML algorithms will be capable of understanding and interpreting user intent with unprecedented accuracy. This will be achieved through the continuous learning from vast datasets, allowing search engines to refine their understanding of context and semantics over time. As these algorithms become more adept at recognizing patterns and nuances, the precision and relevance of search results will reach new heights.

Another exciting development on the horizon is the use of quantum computing to enhance semantic search capabilities. Quantum computers have the potential to process information at speeds far beyond the reach of classical computers, enabling the rapid analysis of complex data sets. In the context of semantic search, quantum computing could revolutionize the way search engines handle large volumes of unstructured data, such as multimedia content and natural language text. By leveraging quantum algorithms, search

31

engines could quickly identify intricate relationships and connections inside data, providing users with more comprehensive and insightful results.

The advent of the Internet of Things (IoT) is also set to impact the future of semantic search. As the number of interconnected devices continues to grow, the volume of data generated by IoT devices will expand exponentially. Semantic search engines will need to adapt to this influx of data by developing methods to effectively index and retrieve information from diverse sources. Innovations in edge computing and data fusion techniques will play a pivotal role in this regard, enabling search engines to process and analyze data closer to its source. This will result in faster retrieval times and more contextually relevant search outcomes, particularly in real-time applications such as smart homes and connected vehicles.

Natural language processing (NLP) is another area where significant advancements are anticipated. Future NLP models will possess a deeper understanding of human language, including idiomatic expressions, cultural references, and emotional nuances. This enhanced linguistic comprehension will enable semantic search engines to better interpret complex queries and provide more accurate responses. Additionally, advancements in NLP will facilitate the development of multilingual search engines capable of seamlessly handling queries in multiple languages. This will be particularly beneficial in our increasingly globalized world, where users often seek information across linguistic boundaries.

The rise of voice-activated search is another trend set to shape the future of semantic search. With the proliferation of voice-activated assistants and smart speakers, users are increasingly relying on voice commands to perform searches. Future semantic search engines will need to excel in understanding and processing spoken language, including accents, dialects, and colloquial expressions. Innovations in speech recognition and voice synthesis technologies will be crucial in this regard, ensuring that search engines can accurately interpret and respond to voice queries. As voice-activated search becomes more prevalent, the user experience will become more seamless and intuitive, further driving the adoption of semantic search.

Personalization is another key trend that will influence the future of semantic search. As users become more accustomed to personalized experiences in their digital interactions, the demand for tailored search results will continue to grow. Future semantic search engines will leverage advanced user profiling and behavioral analysis techniques to deliver highly personalized results. By understanding individual preferences, search history, and contextual factors, search engines will be able to provide results that are uniquely relevant to each user. This level of personalization will enhance user satisfaction and engagement, making semantic search an indispensable tool in various domains.

The integration of semantic search with augmented reality (AR) and virtual reality (VR) technologies is also expected to bring about exciting innovations. As AR and VR applications become more widespread, the need for effective information retrieval inside immersive environments will become increasingly important. Future semantic search engines will be designed to operate seamlessly inside AR and VR interfaces, allowing users to perform searches and access information in a more intuitive and interactive manner. This will open up new possibilities for applications in fields such as education, entertainment, and healthcare, where immersive experiences can greatly enhance the value of retrieved information.

Ethical considerations and responsible AI are also expected to play a significant role in the future of semantic search. As search engines become more powerful and pervasive, ensuring fairness, transparency, and accountability in their operations will be paramount. Future developments will likely focus on creating ethical frameworks and guidelines for the design and deployment of semantic search systems. This will involve addressing issues such as bias in AI algorithms, data privacy, and the responsible use of user data. By prioritizing ethical considerations, the industry can build trust and ensure that semantic search technologies are used for the benefit of society as a whole.

To sum it up, the future of semantic search is brimming with potential for innovation and growth. Advancements in AI and ML, quantum computing, IoT integration, NLP, voice-activated search, personalization, AR and VR integration, and ethical considerations are all poised to shape the next generation of semantic search engines. These trends and innovations will enhance the accuracy, relevance, and user experience of semantic search, making it an even more powerful tool for information retrieval in the years to come. As we continue to explore and develop these technologies, the transformative impact of semantic search will undoubtedly expand, further revolutionizing the way we access and utilize information in our increasingly digital world.

Natural Language Processing Fundamentals For Semantic Search

Introduction to Natural Language Processing (NLP)

In artificial intelligence and machine learning, Natural Language Processing (NLP) stands as a cornerstone technology that bridges the gap between human communication and computer understanding. NLP encompasses a wide array of techniques and methodologies aimed at enabling machines to interpret, generate, and respond to human language in a meaningful way. This section delves into the foundational aspects of NLP, setting the stage for a deeper exploration into its application in Semantic Search.

At its core, NLP involves the interaction between computers and humans using natural language. This interaction is complex because human language is inherently ambiguous and context-dependent. Words can have multiple meanings, and the intended meaning often relies heavily on context, tone, and cultural nuances. Therefore, one of the primary challenges in NLP is to develop algorithms that can accurately discern and process these subtleties.

The history of NLP can be traced back to the 1950s, with early attempts at machine translation and text parsing. Over the decades, significant advancements have been made, driven by the evolution of computational power and the availability of large datasets. Modern NLP leverages sophisticated models and techniques, including machine learning, deep learning, and neural networks, to achieve remarkable levels of accuracy and functionality.

A fundamental concept in NLP is tokenization, which involves breaking down text into smaller units called tokens. These tokens can be words, phrases, or even characters, depending on the level of granularity required. Tokenization is the first step in many NLP tasks, as it transforms raw text into a structured format that can be analyzed and processed by algorithms. For instance, in a sentence like "The quick brown fox jumps over the lazy dog," tokenization would split the sentence into individual words or tokens: ["The", "quick", "brown", "fox", "jumps", "over", "the", "lazy", "dog"].

Once text is tokenized, the next step often involves part-of-speech (POS) tagging, where each token is assigned a grammatical category such as noun, verb, adjective, etc. POS tagging helps in understanding the syntactic structure of a sentence, which is crucial for tasks like parsing and named entity recognition (NER). NER is another essential technique in NLP that identifies and classifies entities inside a text into predefined categories such as names of people, organizations, locations, dates, and more.

Parsing, or syntactic analysis, is the process of analyzing the grammatical structure of a sentence. It involves determining the relationships between tokens, such as which words are the subject or object of a verb. Parsing can be performed using different approaches, including dependency parsing and constituency parsing, each providing a different representation of the sentence structure. Dependency parsing, for instance, focuses on the relationships between words, forming a tree structure where each node represents a word, and edges represent dependencies between them.

Another critical aspect of NLP is semantic analysis, which goes beyond syntactic structure to understand the meaning of text. Semantic analysis involves tasks such as word sense disambiguation, which aims to determine the correct meaning of a word based on context, and sentiment analysis, which assesses the emotional tone of a piece of text. These tasks are vital for applications like sentiment classification in social media posts or customer reviews.

Machine learning plays a pivotal role in modern NLP, with supervised and unsupervised learning techniques being widely used. Supervised learning involves training models on labeled data, where the desired output is known, while unsupervised learning deals with unlabeled data, aiming to discover hidden patterns and relationships. Techniques such as clustering and topic modeling fall under the umbrella of unsupervised learning, providing insights into the structure and themes inside large text corpora.

Deep learning, a subset of machine learning, has revolutionized NLP with the advent of neural networks and models such as recurrent neural networks (RNNs) and transformers. RNNs are designed to handle sequential data, making them well-suited for tasks like language modeling and machine translation. Transformers, on the other hand, have gained prominence due to their ability to handle long-range dependencies and parallelize training, leading to the development of powerful models like BERT (Bidirectional Encoder Representations from Transformers) and GPT (Generative Pre-trained Transformer).

The integration of NLP in Semantic Search enhances the search experience by enabling more intuitive and context-aware retrieval of information. Semantic Search leverages NLP techniques to understand the intent behind a query, rather than relying solely on keyword matching. This results in more relevant and accurate search results, as the system can interpret the nuances of human language and provide answers that align with the user's intent.

In conclusion, Natural Language Processing is a multifaceted field that encompasses a wide range of techniques and methodologies aimed at enabling machines to understand and interact with human language. From tokenization and POS tagging to semantic analysis and deep learning, NLP provides the foundation for advanced applications like Semantic Search. As we continue to explore the intricacies of NLP, it becomes evident that this technology is not just about processing text, but about bridging the gap between human communication and machine understanding, paving the way for more intelligent and intuitive interactions.

Tokenization and text normalization are foundational processes in Natural Language Processing (NLP). These techniques play a crucial role in preparing text data for further analysis and are essential steps in the pipeline of any NLP application, including Semantic Search. This section delves into the various methods and best practices associated with tokenization and text normalization, highlighting their significance and implementation.

Tokenization is the process of dividing text into smaller, manageable units called tokens. These tokens can be words, subwords, or characters, depending on the granularity required for a given task. Tokenization is a critical step because it transforms unstructured text into a structured format that algorithms can process. There are several approaches to tokenization, each with its advantages and challenges.

One of the simplest forms of tokenization is word tokenization, where text is split into individual words based on spaces and punctuation. While straightforward, this method can be problematic for languages that do not use spaces to separate words, such as Chinese or Japanese. Additionally, word tokenization may struggle with handling contractions and possessives in English, requiring additional preprocessing steps.

Subword tokenization offers a more flexible approach by breaking text into smaller units than words. This method is particularly useful for handling out-of-vocabulary words and morphologically rich languages. Byte Pair Encoding (BPE) and WordPiece are popular subword tokenization techniques. BPE iteratively merges the most frequent pairs of characters or character sequences, creating a vocabulary of subwords. WordPiece, on the other hand, uses a similar approach but focuses on maximizing the likelihood of the training data.

Character tokenization takes an even finer-grained approach by treating each character as a token. This method is beneficial for languages with complex morphology or for tasks requiring detailed text analysis. However, it can lead to longer sequences and increased computational complexity, making it less practical for some applications.

Once text is tokenized, the next step is text normalization. Text normalization aims to standardize the text, ensuring consistency and reducing variability. This process involves several techniques, each addressing different aspects of text preprocessing.

Lowercasing is a common normalization technique that converts all characters in the text to lowercase. This step helps reduce the number of unique tokens by treating "Apple" and "apple" as the same word. However, it may not be suitable for tasks where case sensitivity is important, such as named entity recognition.

Removing punctuation and special characters is another essential normalization step. Punctuation marks and special characters can introduce noise into the data, affecting the performance of NLP models. Stripping these characters from the text can help create cleaner and more consistent tokens. However, care must be taken to preserve meaningful punctuation, such as apostrophes in contractions or hyphens in compound words.

Stopword removal involves eliminating common words that carry little semantic value, such as "and," "the," and "is." These words, known as stopwords, can inflate the size of the vocabulary and hinder the performance of NLP models. Removing stopwords can help focus the analysis on more informative words. However, the decision to remove stopwords should be task-specific, as they may carry important context in some applications.

Stemming and lemmatization are advanced normalization techniques that aim to reduce words to their base or root form. Stemming uses heuristic rules to strip affixes from words, resulting in a crude approximation of the root form. For example, stemming might reduce "running," "runner," and "ran" to the root "run." Lemmatization, on the other hand, uses linguistic knowledge to map words to their canonical form, considering the word's part of speech and context. While lemmatization is more accurate than stemming, it requires more computational resources and language-specific knowledge.

Handling numbers and numerical expressions is another aspect of text normalization. Numbers can be represented in various formats, such as digits, words, or a combination of both. Standardizing numerical expressions can help improve the consistency of the text. For example, converting "twenty-one" to "21" or normalizing dates to a standard format can facilitate better analysis and comparison.

Dealing with misspellings and typographical errors is also crucial for text normalization. Spelling correction algorithms, such as edit distance or phonetic matching, can help identify and correct common misspellings. Ensuring that words are correctly spelled and standardized can significantly enhance the quality of the text data.

In the context of Semantic Search, tokenization and text normalization are indispensable for understanding and processing user queries and documents. Accurate tokenization ensures that the text is broken down into meaningful units, while effective normalization techniques standardize the text, reducing variability and noise. These processes enable more accurate and relevant search results by allowing the system to interpret and match queries with the underlying content more effectively.

In summary, tokenization and text normalization are fundamental steps in the NLP pipeline, crucial for preparing text data for analysis. Various tokenization techniques, from word to character level, offer different levels of granularity and flexibility. Text normalization techniques, such as lowercasing, punctuation removal, stopword elimination, stemming, lemmatization, and spelling correction, ensure consistency and reduce noise. Together, these processes lay the groundwork for advanced NLP applications, including Semantic Search, by facilitating accurate and meaningful text analysis.

In the landscape of Natural Language Processing (NLP), the processes of Part-of-Speech (POS) tagging and Named Entity Recognition (NER) are essential for understanding and interpreting text. These techniques enable machines to gain a deeper comprehension of the structure and meaning of language, which is pivotal for enhancing the accuracy and relevance of Semantic Search.

Part-of-Speech tagging is a method used to assign grammatical categories to individual words in a sentence. This categorization helps in understanding the syntactic structure and the functional role of each word. For example, in the sentence "She enjoys reading books," POS tagging would classify "She" as a pronoun, "enjoys" as a verb, "reading" as a gerund, and "books" as a noun. By doing so, the system can decipher the relationships between words, facilitating more sophisticated text analysis.

The process of POS tagging involves several steps. Initially, the text is tokenized, breaking it down into individual words or tokens. Once tokenized, each word is analyzed inside its context to determine its part of speech. This analysis can be performed using various algorithms, ranging from rule-based approaches to machine learning models. Rule-based systems rely on predefined linguistic rules to assign tags, while machine learning models use statistical methods to predict tags based on patterns observed in the training data.

One of the challenges in POS tagging is handling words that can belong to multiple categories depending on the context. For instance, the word "run" can be a verb ("I run every morning") or a noun ("He went for a run"). Advanced POS taggers leverage contextual information and probabilistic models to disambiguate such cases, achieving higher accuracy.

Named Entity Recognition (NER) is another critical technique in NLP, focusing on identifying and classifying entities inside text. Entities can be names of people, organizations, locations, dates, and more. NER enhances the understanding of text by highlighting significant elements, making it easier to extract relevant information and perform tasks such as information retrieval, question answering, and summarization.

The process of NER involves several stages. Initially, the text is preprocessed to remove noise and standardize the format. Following this, the text is tokenized, and each token is analyzed to determine if it represents an entity. This analysis can be performed using various approaches, including dictionary-based methods, rule-based systems, and machine learning models. Dictionary-based methods rely on predefined lists of entities, while rule-based systems use linguistic patterns to identify entities. Machine learning models, on the other hand, learn to recognize entities from annotated training data, making them more adaptable and accurate.

One of the challenges in NER is dealing with entities that have multiple forms or variations. For example, "New York" can appear as "NYC," "New York City," or "NY." Advanced NER systems use techniques such as fuzzy matching and context analysis to handle such variations, ensuring that all forms of an entity are correctly identified.

Both POS tagging and NER play a vital role in Semantic Search by providing a deeper understanding of the text. POS tagging helps in parsing the syntactic structure of queries

44

and documents, enabling the system to recognize the relationships between words and phrases. This understanding allows the search engine to interpret complex queries more accurately and retrieve relevant results.

NER, on the other hand, enhances the search experience by identifying and highlighting key entities inside the text. By recognizing entities, the search engine can provide more targeted and relevant results. For example, if a user searches for "best restaurants in Paris," an NER system can identify "Paris" as a location and focus the search on restaurants in that city, rather than returning irrelevant results.

The integration of POS tagging and NER in Semantic Search systems also enables advanced features such as query expansion and entity linking. Query expansion involves automatically adding related terms to a user's query to improve search results. For instance, if a user searches for "Apple," the system can use NER to determine whether the user is referring to the fruit or the technology company and expand the query accordingly. Entity linking involves connecting entities mentioned in the text to their corresponding entries in a knowledge base, providing additional context and information.

In the end, Part-of-Speech tagging and Named Entity Recognition are fundamental techniques in Natural Language Processing that significantly enhance the capabilities of Semantic Search systems. By understanding the grammatical structure and identifying key entities inside text, these techniques enable more accurate and relevant search results. As NLP continues to evolve, the integration of POS tagging and NER will play an increasingly important role in bridging the gap between human language and machine understanding, paving the way for more intelligent and intuitive search experiences.

Understanding the structural aspects of language is crucial for advanced Natural Language Processing (NLP) tasks, particularly in the context of Semantic Search. Two fundamental techniques that facilitate this understanding are Dependency Parsing and Constituency Parsing. These methods provide insights into the grammatical relationships and hierarchical structure of sentences, respectively, allowing machines to interpret and process text more effectively. This section delves into the intricacies of these parsing techniques, their applications, and their significance in enhancing Semantic Search systems.

Dependency Parsing is a technique that focuses on the relationships between words in a sentence. It aims to represent the syntactic structure by identifying dependencies among words, where each word is connected to its dependents through directed links. These links, or dependencies, indicate how words modify or complement each other, forming a tree structure known as a dependency tree. In this tree, each node represents a word, and an edge signifies the dependency relation between the words.

For instance, consider the sentence "The cat chased the mouse." In a dependency tree, "chased" would be the root verb, with "cat" as its subject and "mouse" as its object. The article "The" would be linked to "cat" and "mouse" as determiners. This representation helps in understanding who did what to whom, providing a clear picture of the sentence's grammatical structure.

Dependency Parsing is particularly useful in Semantic Search because it helps in grasping the intent and meaning behind user queries. By analyzing the dependencies, the system can discern the focus of a query and retrieve more relevant results. For example, in the query "books written by George Orwell," dependency parsing can identify "books" as the main subject and "George Orwell" as the author, thereby prioritizing search results that match this specific relationship.

Several algorithms and models are employed for Dependency Parsing, ranging from rule-based systems to machine learning approaches. Rule-based systems rely on predefined grammatical rules to identify dependencies, while machine learning models, such as transition-based parsers and graph-based parsers, use annotated corpora to learn and predict dependencies. Transition-based parsers build the dependency tree incrementally by making a series of parsing decisions, whereas graph-based parsers consider all possible dependencies simultaneously and select the most likely structure.

Constituency Parsing, on the other hand, focuses on the hierarchical structure of a sentence by dividing it into sub-phrases or constituents. This technique represents the sentence as a constituency tree, where each node corresponds to a phrase or a word, and the branches denote the relationships between these constituents. The tree's root represents the entire sentence, and it is recursively broken down into smaller constituents, such as noun phrases (NP), verb phrases (VP), and prepositional phrases (PP).

For example, in the sentence "The quick brown fox jumps over the lazy dog," a constituency tree would have the entire sentence as the root, which is then split into a noun phrase "The quick brown fox" and a verb phrase "jumps over the lazy dog." The noun phrase can further be divided into the determiner "The" and the noun "quick brown fox," while the verb phrase can be split into the verb "jumps" and the prepositional phrase "over the lazy dog." This hierarchical representation helps in understanding the sentence's structure and the relationships between different phrases.

Constituency Parsing is valuable in Semantic Search as it aids in comprehending complex queries and extracting meaningful information. By analyzing the hierarchical structure, the system can identify key phrases and their roles, enabling more accurate interpretation and retrieval. For instance, in the query "best Italian restaurants in New York," constituency parsing can separate "best Italian restaurants" as the main subject and "in New York" as the location, thereby refining the search results to match the user's intent.

Various algorithms and models are used for Constituency Parsing, including probabilistic context-free grammars (PCFGs), lexicalized parsing, and neural network-based approaches. PCFGs extend context-free grammars by associating probabilities with grammar rules, allowing the parser to select the most likely tree structure. Lexicalized parsing enhances PCFGs by incorporating lexical information, such as word dependencies and headwords, improving the parser's accuracy. Neural network-based approaches leverage deep learning techniques, such as recurrent neural networks (RNNs) and transformers, to capture long-range dependencies and contextual information, achieving state-of-the-art performance in Constituency Parsing.

Both Dependency Parsing and Constituency Parsing offer unique advantages and can be complementary in NLP applications. Dependency Parsing excels in capturing the direct relationships between words, making it suitable for tasks that require fine-grained syntactic analysis, such as relation extraction and sentiment analysis. Constituency Parsing, with its hierarchical representation, is well-suited for tasks that involve understanding the overall structure of sentences, such as text summarization and question answering.

In Semantic Search, combining both parsing techniques can lead to more robust and accurate systems. Dependency Parsing can help in identifying the core elements and their relationships in a query, while Constituency Parsing can provide a broader understanding of the sentence structure. This combination enables the search engine to interpret queries more precisely and deliver results that are closely aligned with the user's intent.

To sum it up, Dependency Parsing and Constituency Parsing are fundamental techniques in Natural Language Processing that play a crucial role in understanding and interpreting text. Dependency Parsing focuses on the relationships between words, representing the syntactic structure through dependency trees, while Constituency Parsing emphasizes the hierarchical structure, breaking sentences into sub-phrases. Both techniques offer significant benefits for Semantic Search, enhancing the system's ability to comprehend complex queries and retrieve relevant results. By leveraging these parsing methods, Semantic Search systems can achieve a deeper understanding of language, leading to more intelligent and intuitive search experiences.

In Natural Language Processing (NLP), one of the most transformative advancements has been the development of word embeddings. These dense vector representations of words capture semantic relationships and contextual nuances, facilitating more sophisticated and meaningful text analysis. This section delves into the foundational concepts of word embeddings, focusing on prominent models such as Word2Vec and GloVe, and explores advancements that have extended these techniques.

Word embeddings are a type of distributed representation where words are mapped to continuous vector spaces. Unlike traditional one-hot encoding, which represents words as sparse vectors with high dimensionality, word embeddings condense this information into dense vectors of lower dimensions. This compact representation is advantageous because it captures semantic relationships between words, enabling models to understand and process text more effectively.

One of the pioneering approaches to generating word embeddings is Word2Vec, developed by a team of researchers at Google led by Tomas Mikolov. Word2Vec employs neural networks to learn word representations from large corpora of text. It offers two main architectures: Continuous Bag of Words (CBOW) and Skip-gram.

The CBOW model predicts a target word based on its surrounding context words. For instance, given a sentence, the model attempts to predict a missing word by considering the words around it. This approach helps the model learn the context in which words appear, capturing the semantic relationships between them. Conversely, the Skip-gram model works in the opposite manner. It predicts the context words given a target word, aiming to maximize the probability of context words appearing in the vicinity of the target. This method is particularly effective for capturing the meaning of rare words, as it leverages the context provided by more frequent words.

Both CBOW and Skip-gram use a simple neural network with a single hidden layer to learn the word vectors. During training, the network adjusts the weights to minimize the error in predicting the target or context words. These weights ultimately become the word embeddings, encapsulating the semantic information of words in a continuous vector space. One of the key strengths of Word2Vec is its ability to capture linear relationships between words. For example, the vector representation of "king" minus "man" plus "woman" results in a vector close to "queen," illustrating how the model encodes semantic relationships.

Despite its success, Word2Vec has some limitations. It focuses on local context and may not capture long-range dependencies between words. Additionally, it relies on a fixed window size for context, which might not be optimal for all types of text.

To address some of these limitations, researchers at Stanford introduced GloVe (Global Vectors for Word Representation). Unlike Word2Vec, which relies on local context windows, GloVe leverages global word co-occurrence statistics to learn word embeddings. The central idea behind GloVe is that the ratio of word-word co-occurrence probabilities can encode semantic relationships.

GloVe constructs a co-occurrence matrix, where each entry represents the frequency with which a pair of words appears together in a large corpus. This matrix is then factorized to obtain word vectors that capture the statistical information. By focusing on the global context, GloVe embeddings can capture broader semantic relationships that might be missed by models relying solely on local context.

One of the distinguishing features of GloVe is its ability to handle both frequent and rare words effectively. The model balances the influence of frequent words while still capturing meaningful relationships for less common words. Moreover, GloVe embeddings exhibit linear substructures, similar to Word2Vec, enabling analogical reasoning. For example, the relationship between "Paris" and "France" is similar to that between "Tokyo" and "Japan."

While Word2Vec and GloVe have been instrumental in advancing NLP, the field has continued to evolve, leading to more sophisticated models that build upon these foundations. One notable advancement is the introduction of contextualized word embeddings, exemplified by models such as ELMo (Embeddings from Language Models) and BERT (Bidirectional Encoder Representations from Transformers).

Contextualized word embeddings differ from traditional embeddings in that they generate dynamic representations based on the context in which words appear. This approach addresses the limitation of static embeddings, where a word has a single vector representation regardless of its context. For instance, the word "bank" has different meanings in the sentences "He sat by the river bank" and "She went to the bank to deposit money." Contextualized embeddings capture these nuances by generating different vectors for the word "bank" based on its surrounding context.

ELMo, developed by researchers at Allen Institute for AI, is one of the pioneering models in this category. It uses a deep bidirectional language model to generate word representations. The model is trained to predict the next word in a sentence, considering both the left and right context. By incorporating information from both directions, ELMo captures richer contextual information, resulting in more accurate word representations. These embeddings are particularly effective for tasks that require understanding the syntactic and semantic nuances of language, such as named entity recognition and sentiment analysis.

BERT, introduced by researchers at Google, takes the concept of contextualized embeddings further by employing a transformer-based architecture. Unlike previous models, BERT is designed to pre-train deep bidirectional representations by jointly conditioning on both left and right context in all layers. This pre-training is followed by fine-tuning on specific tasks, allowing BERT to achieve state-of-the-art performance in a wide range of NLP applications.

BERT's architecture consists of multiple layers of transformers, which are capable of capturing long-range dependencies and complex relationships between words. During pre-training, BERT uses two tasks: masked language modeling and next sentence prediction. In masked language modeling, random words in a sentence are masked, and the model is trained to predict the masked words based on the surrounding context. In next sentence prediction, the model learns to predict whether a given sentence follows another, enabling it to capture relationships between sentences.

The success of BERT has spurred the development of even more advanced models, such as GPT (Generative Pre-trained Transformer) and T5 (Text-to-Text Transfer Transformer). These models build upon the principles of pre-training and fine-tuning, pushing the boundaries of what is possible with word embeddings and contextualized representations.

Conclusively, word embeddings have revolutionized the field of Natural Language Processing, enabling models to capture semantic relationships and contextual information in a compact and meaningful manner. From the foundational models like Word2Vec and GloVe to the more advanced contextualized embeddings of ELMo and BERT, these techniques have significantly enhanced our ability to process and understand text. As the field continues to evolve, we can expect further innovations that will push the boundaries of what is possible, driving the development of more sophisticated and effective Semantic Search systems.

The evolution of Natural Language Processing (NLP) has been marked by significant milestones, with one of the most transformative being the advent of transformers and attention mechanisms. These innovations have revolutionized the way machines understand and generate human language, enabling more sophisticated and context-aware text processing. In this section, we will explore the fundamental concepts of transformers and attention mechanisms, their applications, and their implications for Semantic Search.

Transformers represent a paradigm shift in NLP, offering a novel architecture that addresses the limitations of traditional sequence models. Prior to transformers, models such as Recurrent Neural Networks (RNNs) and Long Short-Term Memory (LSTM) networks were commonly used for sequential data. While effective, these models struggled with capturing long-range dependencies due to their sequential nature, leading to issues like vanishing gradients and inefficiencies in parallel processing.

The transformer architecture, introduced by Vaswani et al. in their seminal paper "Attention is All You Need," overcomes these challenges by leveraging self-attention mechanisms. Unlike RNNs and LSTMs, transformers do not process data sequentially. Instead, they employ a mechanism that allows each word in a sentence to attend to every other word, irrespective of their positions. This parallelism not only improves computational efficiency but also enhances the model's ability to capture long-range dependencies and contextual relationships.

At the core of the transformer architecture is the self-attention mechanism, which computes attention scores for each word with respect to all other words in the sequence. These scores determine the importance of each word in the context of the others, enabling the model to focus on relevant information. The self-attention mechanism operates through three key components: queries, keys, and values. Each word in the sequence is represented by these components, and the attention scores are computed by taking the dot product of the queries and keys, followed by a softmax operation to obtain attention weights. These weights are then used to generate weighted sums of the values, producing the final attention output.

The transformer model consists of an encoder-decoder structure, with both components comprising multiple layers of self-attention and feed-forward neural networks. The encoder processes the input sequence, generating contextualized representations for each word. These representations are then passed to the decoder, which generates the output sequence, one word at a time. This architecture is highly versatile and can be adapted for various NLP tasks, including machine translation, text summarization, and language modeling.

One of the key advantages of transformers is their scalability. The parallel processing capability of transformers allows them to handle large datasets and complex tasks more efficiently than traditional models. This scalability has paved the way for the development of large-scale pre-trained language models, such as BERT (Bidirectional Encoder Representations from Transformers) and GPT (Generative Pre-trained Transformer). These models leverage transformers to learn rich contextual representations from vast amounts of text data, achieving state-of-the-art performance on a wide range of NLP benchmarks.

Attention mechanisms, a fundamental component of transformers, have also played a crucial role in advancing NLP. The concept of attention was first introduced in the context of neural machine translation by Bahdanau et al., who proposed an attention-based model that allowed the decoder to focus on relevant parts of the input sequence. This approach significantly improved translation quality by enabling the model to dynamically weigh the importance of different words in the source sentence.

Building on this idea, self-attention mechanisms in transformers extend the concept by allowing each word to attend to all other words in the sequence, regardless of their positions. This global attention enables the model to capture intricate relationships and dependencies, making it particularly effective for tasks that require a deep understanding of context. For example, in sentiment analysis, self-attention mechanisms can help the model discern subtle nuances in sentiment by considering the interactions between words across the entire sentence.

The impact of transformers and attention mechanisms on Semantic Search is profound. Traditional search engines rely on keyword matching and heuristic-based ranking algorithms, which often fall short in understanding the nuanced meanings of user queries. By incorporating transformers, Semantic Search systems can achieve a more sophisticated understanding of language, leading to more accurate and relevant search results.

Transformers enhance Semantic Search by enabling contextualized query understanding. Unlike keyword-based approaches, where the presence of specific terms determines relevance, transformers analyze the entire query in context, capturing the underlying intent. For instance, a search query like "best place to visit in autumn" can be interpreted more accurately by considering the relationships between words, allowing the search engine to prioritize results that align with the user's intent.

Moreover, transformers facilitate advanced features such as query expansion and semantic matching. Query expansion involves augmenting the original query with related terms to improve recall. Transformers can generate contextually relevant expansions by analyzing the relationships between words, enhancing the search engine's ability to retrieve comprehensive results. Semantic matching, on the other hand, involves comparing the query with documents at a semantic level, rather than relying solely on keyword overlap. Transformers enable this by generating rich vector representations for both queries and documents, allowing for more precise matching based on meaning.

The versatility of transformers extends to various applications inside Semantic Search, including document ranking, snippet generation, and question answering. In document ranking, transformers can evaluate the relevance of documents by considering the entire context of the query and the document, leading to more accurate rankings. For snippet generation, transformers can extract the most relevant sections of a document that directly address the user's query, providing concise and informative summaries. In question answering, transformers can comprehend complex questions and generate precise answers by attending to relevant parts of the context.

Despite their remarkable capabilities, transformers are not without challenges. One of the primary concerns is their computational cost. The self-attention mechanism, while powerful, requires significant computational resources, especially for long sequences. This has led to ongoing research efforts aimed at developing more efficient variants of transformers, such as the Transformer-XL and the Reformer, which address issues related to memory and computational efficiency.

Another challenge is the interpretability of transformer models. While transformers excel at capturing complex relationships, their inner workings can be difficult to interpret. This opacity raises concerns about the transparency and accountability of AI systems, particularly in applications where understanding the decision-making process is crucial. Researchers are actively exploring methods to improve the interpretability of transformers, such as attention visualization techniques and probing tasks that shed light on the information captured by different layers.

In essence, transformers and attention mechanisms have revolutionized NLP, offering powerful tools for understanding and generating human language. Their impact on Semantic Search is transformative, enabling more accurate, context-aware, and relevant search experiences. As research in this field continues to advance, we can expect further innovations that will push the boundaries of what is possible, driving the development of more intelligent and intuitive search systems. The journey of transformers in NLP is a testament to the profound potential of attention mechanisms, and their continued evolution promises to shape the future of language understanding and search technology.

Understanding the emotional tone and categorizing text into predefined labels are critical tasks in Natural Language Processing (NLP) that significantly enhance the capabilities of Semantic Search systems. Sentiment Analysis and Text Classification are two fundamental techniques that enable machines to interpret user intent, discern emotions, and categorize content effectively. This section explores these techniques, their methodologies, and their applications in improving Semantic Search.

Sentiment Analysis, also known as opinion mining, involves determining the sentiment expressed in a piece of text. It identifies whether the sentiment is positive, negative, or neutral, providing valuable insights into user opinions and emotions. This technique is widely used in various applications, including social media monitoring, customer feedback analysis, and brand reputation management.

The process of Sentiment Analysis typically begins with data preprocessing, where the text is cleaned and normalized. This involves removing noise such as special characters, numbers, and stop words, as well as converting the text to lowercase to ensure uniformity. Tokenization is then performed to split the text into individual words or tokens, which serve as the basic units for analysis.

Once the text is preprocessed, feature extraction techniques are employed to represent the text in a format suitable for machine learning algorithms. Bag-of-Words (BoW) and Term Frequency-Inverse Document Frequency (TF-IDF) are common methods for feature extraction. BoW represents the text as a vector of word counts, while TF-IDF assigns a weight to each word based on its frequency in the document and its inverse frequency across all documents. These representations capture the importance of words in conveying sentiment.

Machine learning algorithms play a pivotal role in Sentiment Analysis. Supervised learning techniques, such as Naive Bayes, Support Vector Machines (SVM), and logistic regression, are often used to build sentiment classifiers. These algorithms are trained on labeled datasets, where the sentiment of each text is known. During training, the algorithms learn to associate specific features with positive, negative, or neutral sentiments. Once trained, the models can predict the sentiment of new, unseen text.

Deep learning approaches, particularly those involving neural networks, have also shown remarkable performance in Sentiment Analysis. Convolutional Neural Networks (CNNs) and Recurrent Neural Networks (RNNs) are commonly used architectures. CNNs are effective in capturing local patterns in text, while RNNs, especially Long Short-Term Memory (LSTM) networks, excel at modeling sequential dependencies. These networks can automatically learn features from raw text data, eliminating the need for manual feature extraction.

Sentiment Analysis has numerous applications in enhancing Semantic Search. For instance, in e-commerce, understanding customer reviews' sentiment can help in ranking products based on user satisfaction. In social media platforms, analyzing sentiment in user posts can aid in identifying trending topics and gauging public opinion. By incorporating sentiment information, Semantic Search systems can deliver more relevant and emotionally resonant results.

Text Classification, on the other hand, involves categorizing text into predefined classes or categories. This technique is essential for organizing and managing large volumes of text data, enabling efficient retrieval and analysis. Text Classification is used in various applications, including spam detection, topic categorization, and document indexing.

The process of Text Classification shares similarities with Sentiment Analysis, starting with data preprocessing and feature extraction. However, the focus here is on representing the text in a way that captures the information relevant to the classification task. In addition to BoW and TF-IDF, word embeddings are often used for feature representation in Text Classification. Word embeddings, such as Word2Vec and GloVe, represent words as dense vectors in a continuous space, capturing semantic relationships and contextual information.

Supervised learning algorithms are commonly used for Text Classification. Decision trees, random forests, and SVMs are popular choices for building classifiers. These algorithms are trained on labeled datasets, where each text is associated with a specific category. During training, the algorithms learn to map features to categories, enabling them to classify new text accurately.

Deep learning techniques have also revolutionized Text Classification. Neural networks, particularly CNNs and RNNs, have demonstrated superior performance in various classification tasks. CNNs can capture local dependencies and hierarchical patterns in text, while RNNs, with their ability to model sequential data, are well-suited for tasks involving context and order. Transformer-based models, such as BERT and GPT, have further advanced Text Classification by leveraging attention mechanisms to capture long-range dependencies and contextual nuances.

Text Classification has numerous applications in improving Semantic Search. For example, in news aggregators, classifying articles into topics such as politics, sports, and technology allows users to find relevant content quickly. In email filtering, classifying emails as spam or non-spam enhances the user experience by reducing clutter. By integrating Text Classification, Semantic Search systems can provide more organized and targeted search results.

To sum it up, Sentiment Analysis and Text Classification are fundamental techniques in NLP that play a crucial role in enhancing Semantic Search. Sentiment Analysis enables the interpretation of emotional tone, providing insights into user opinions and preferences. Text Classification facilitates the organization and categorization of text, enabling efficient retrieval and analysis. By leveraging these techniques, Semantic Search systems can deliver more relevant, emotionally resonant, and organized results, significantly improving the user experience.

Building Semantic Search Models: Techniques And Tools

Introduction to Building Semantic Search Models

In the evolving landscape of information retrieval, semantic search has emerged as a powerful paradigm shift from traditional keyword-based search methodologies. The essence of semantic search lies in its ability to understand the intent and contextual meaning behind search queries, thereby delivering more accurate and relevant results. This section delves into the foundational aspects of constructing semantic search models, exploring the techniques and tools that form the bedrock of this advanced search technology.

To begin with, it is essential to comprehend the fundamental principles that underpin semantic search. Unlike conventional search engines that rely heavily on keyword matching, semantic search leverages the understanding of natural language to interpret the meaning of words and phrases inside a given context. This involves the use of sophisticated algorithms that can discern relationships between terms, recognize synonyms, and even decode the nuances of human language.

One of the pivotal techniques in building semantic search models is the use of embeddings. Embeddings are dense vector representations of words or phrases that capture their meanings in a high-dimensional space. These vectors are generated through various methods, such as Word2Vec, GloVe, and fastText, each offering unique advantages in capturing semantic relationships. For instance, Word2Vec creates embeddings by analyzing the context in which words appear, thereby enabling the model to understand the similarity between words based on their usage patterns. GloVe, on the other hand, utilizes global word co-occurrence statistics to generate embeddings, providing a broader perspective on word relationships.

Another critical aspect of semantic search is the implementation of neural networks, particularly deep learning models. These models, such as Convolutional Neural Networks (CNNs) and Recurrent Neural Networks (RNNs), have demonstrated remarkable efficacy in processing and understanding natural language. CNNs are adept at capturing local dependencies in text, making them suitable for tasks like sentiment analysis and text classification. RNNs, with their ability to maintain contextual information across sequences, are particularly effective in handling sequential data, such as sentences and paragraphs. The advent of transformer-based models, like BERT and GPT, has further revolutionized semantic search by enabling more sophisticated and nuanced understanding of language.

In addition to embeddings and neural networks, the use of ontologies and knowledge graphs plays a significant role in enhancing semantic search. Ontologies provide a structured representation of knowledge inside a particular domain, defining the relationships between concepts and entities. This structured knowledge enables search models to infer connections between terms and understand the hierarchical organization of information. Knowledge graphs, on the other hand, extend this concept by linking entities across diverse domains, creating a web of interconnected information. This interconnectedness allows semantic search models to retrieve information that is contextually relevant and semantically rich.

The process of building semantic search models also involves various preprocessing steps to ensure the quality and relevance of the input data. Text preprocessing techniques, such as tokenization, stemming, and lemmatization, are employed to standardize the text and reduce it to its fundamental components. Tokenization involves breaking down text into individual words or phrases, while stemming and lemmatization reduce words to their root forms. These preprocessing steps are crucial in eliminating noise and ensuring that the semantic search model can focus on the core meaning of the text.

Furthermore, the evaluation of semantic search models is a critical component of the development process. Traditional evaluation metrics, such as precision, recall, and F1-score, are often supplemented with more advanced metrics like Mean Reciprocal Rank (MRR) and Normalized Discounted Cumulative Gain (NDCG). These metrics provide a comprehensive assessment of the model's performance in retrieving relevant information and ranking search results. MRR, for instance, evaluates the rank at which the first relevant result appears, while NDCG considers the quality of the entire ranked list of search results.

The tools and frameworks available for building semantic search models are diverse and continually evolving. Open-source libraries such as TensorFlow, PyTorch, and Hugging Face's Transformers offer robust platforms for developing and deploying semantic search models. TensorFlow provides a comprehensive ecosystem for machine learning and deep learning, with extensive support for building and training neural networks. PyTorch, known for its dynamic computational graph, offers flexibility and ease of use, making it a popular choice among researchers and developers. Hugging Face's Transformers library, with its pre-trained models and easy-to-use APIs, has become a go-to resource for implementing transformer-based models in semantic search.

66

In conclusion, the journey of building semantic search models is a multifaceted endeavor that encompasses a range of techniques and tools. From the generation of embeddings and the implementation of neural networks to the use of ontologies and knowledge graphs, each component plays a vital role in creating a robust and effective semantic search system. The continuous advancements in natural language processing and machine learning are driving the evolution of semantic search, promising ever more accurate and contextually aware search experiences. As we delve deeper into the intricacies of semantic search, it becomes evident that understanding and harnessing these technologies is key to unlocking the full potential of information retrieval in the modern era.

In the realm of developing advanced search models, the initial stages of data collection and preprocessing are paramount. These foundational steps lay the groundwork for creating robust and efficient semantic search systems. This section delves into the intricacies of gathering and refining data, ensuring that it is primed for subsequent modeling stages.

To begin with, data collection is the cornerstone of any semantic search project. The quality and diversity of the data directly influence the performance and accuracy of the search model. Therefore, it is crucial to source data from a variety of repositories to capture a wide range of contexts and meanings. Sources can include digital libraries, web crawlers, public datasets, and proprietary databases. Each source offers unique advantages and challenges, necessitating a strategic approach to data gathering.

When collecting data, it is essential to consider the domain-specific requirements of the semantic search model. For instance, a model designed for medical literature will require datasets rich in medical terminology and context, while a model for legal documents will necessitate a different set of linguistic nuances. Ensuring that the collected data aligns with the intended application domain enhances the relevance and effectiveness of the search model.

Once the data is collected, the next critical step is preprocessing. Preprocessing transforms raw data into a structured format suitable for analysis and modeling. This stage involves several techniques aimed at standardizing and cleaning the data, thus improving its quality and usability.

One of the primary preprocessing tasks is text normalization. This process entails converting text to a consistent format, which often involves lowercasing all words, removing punctuation, and handling special characters. Normalization ensures that variations in text do not lead to discrepancies in the model's interpretation.

Tokenization follows normalization and involves breaking down text into smaller units, such as words or phrases. Tokenization is a critical step as it forms the basis for further text analysis. Depending on the complexity of the language and the requirements of the model, tokenization can be as simple as splitting text by spaces or as sophisticated as identifying multi-word expressions.

Another essential preprocessing technique is stopword removal. Stopwords are common words like "and," "the," and "is," which typically do not carry significant meaning in the context of semantic search. Removing these words helps in reducing noise and focusing the model on more meaningful terms. However, the list of stopwords can be domain-specific, and careful consideration is required to ensure that important words are not inadvertently excluded.

Stemming and lemmatization are additional preprocessing steps that aim to reduce words to their root forms. Stemming involves stripping suffixes from words, which can sometimes lead to non-dictionary forms. Lemmatization, on the other hand, uses linguistic rules to convert words to their base or dictionary form. While stemming is computationally simpler, lemmatization often provides more accurate results, particularly for complex languages.

Handling missing data is another crucial aspect of preprocessing. Incomplete data can lead to biased or inaccurate models, so it is essential to address gaps in the dataset. Techniques for handling missing data include imputation, where missing values are filled in based on statistical methods, and deletion, where incomplete records are removed. The choice of technique depends on the extent of missing data and its impact on the overall dataset.

Data augmentation is a powerful technique to enhance the diversity and quantity of data. This process involves generating new data points by applying transformations to existing data, such as synonym replacement, paraphrasing, and back-translation. Data augmentation helps in creating a more robust and generalizable model by exposing it to a wider range of linguistic variations.

In addition to these techniques, feature extraction is a critical preprocessing step for semantic search models. Feature extraction involves identifying and selecting relevant attributes from the text that can be used as inputs for the model. Common features include term frequency, inverse document frequency, and part-of-speech tags. Advanced feature extraction methods, such as named entity recognition and dependency parsing, provide deeper insights into the structure and meaning of the text.

The final stage of preprocessing is data validation and quality assurance. This involves verifying that the preprocessed data meets the required standards and is free from errors or inconsistencies. Techniques such as cross-validation, data profiling, and anomaly detection are used to ensure the integrity and reliability of the data. Quality assurance is a continuous process, and periodic reviews are necessary to maintain the dataset's accuracy and relevance.

In essence, data collection and preprocessing are critical stages in building effective semantic search models. These steps ensure that the data is of high quality, relevant, and ready for subsequent modeling stages. By carefully sourcing, cleaning, and refining data, developers can create robust and accurate semantic search systems that deliver meaningful and relevant results. The continuous evolution of data preprocessing techniques promises to further enhance the capabilities of semantic search, paving the way for more sophisticated and nuanced information retrieval systems.

The development of deep learning models for semantic search is an intricate and multifaceted endeavor. This section will explore the essential processes and methodologies involved in training these models effectively. It is imperative to understand that the success of a semantic search system hinges on the robustness of its underlying deep learning architecture. The following discussion will provide a comprehensive overview of the key steps, from data preparation to model evaluation, ensuring a thorough grasp of the subject.

To embark on the journey of training deep learning models for semantic search, one must first ensure that the data is meticulously prepared. The significance of high-quality data cannot be overstated, as it forms the bedrock upon which the entire model is built. Data preparation involves several critical steps, each contributing to the creation of a clean and structured dataset. These steps include data cleansing, normalization, tokenization, and feature extraction. By meticulously preparing the data, we lay a solid foundation for the subsequent training process.

Once the data is prepped, the next phase involves selecting an appropriate deep learning architecture. The choice of architecture is pivotal, as it directly impacts the model's ability to understand and interpret natural language. Various architectures have been developed over the years, each offering unique advantages. Among the most prominent are convolutional neural networks (CNNs), recurrent neural networks (RNNs), and transformer-based models. Each of these architectures has its own strengths and is suited to different aspects of semantic search.

Convolutional neural networks (CNNs) have proven to be highly effective in capturing local patterns inside text data. Their ability to identify and leverage local dependencies makes them particularly useful for tasks that involve analyzing short text segments. On the other hand, recurrent neural networks (RNNs), with their inherent ability to maintain contextual information across sequences, are well-suited for tasks that require understanding the temporal dynamics of text. Furthermore, the advent of transformer-based models has revolutionized the field of natural language processing. These models, with their attention mechanisms, excel at capturing long-range dependencies and have set new benchmarks in various language-related tasks.

Once the architecture is selected, the next crucial step is to initialize the model's parameters. Proper initialization is essential to ensure that the model converges effectively during training. Techniques such as Xavier initialization and He initialization are commonly employed to set the initial values of the model's weights. These techniques help in maintaining the stability of the model and prevent issues like vanishing or exploding gradients.

With the model initialized, the training process begins in earnest. Training a deep learning model involves iteratively updating its parameters based on the error between the predicted and actual outputs. This process is guided by an optimization algorithm, with stochastic gradient descent (SGD) being one of the most widely used. Variants of SGD, such as Adam and RMSprop, offer adaptive learning rates and have been shown to accelerate the convergence of deep learning models.

During training, it is essential to monitor the model's performance to ensure that it is learning effectively. This is typically done by evaluating the model on a validation set, which is a subset of the data that is not used for training. Metrics such as loss, accuracy, and precision are commonly used to gauge the model's performance. Additionally, techniques like early stopping can be employed to prevent overfitting, which occurs when the model performs well on the training data but poorly on unseen data.

Another critical aspect of training deep learning models for semantic search is hyperparameter tuning. Hyperparameters, such as learning rate, batch size, and the number of layers, play a significant role in determining the model's performance. Tuning these hyperparameters involves experimenting with different values and selecting the ones that yield the best results. Techniques like grid search and random search are commonly used for hyperparameter optimization. More advanced methods, such as Bayesian optimization, offer a more systematic approach to finding optimal hyperparameters.

Once the model is trained, the next step is to evaluate its performance on a test set. The test set is a separate subset of the data that is used to assess the model's generalization ability. This evaluation provides an unbiased estimate of the model's performance on unseen data. Metrics such as F1-score, mean reciprocal rank (MRR), and normalized discounted cumulative gain (NDCG) are commonly used to evaluate the effectiveness of semantic search models.

In addition to quantitative evaluation, qualitative analysis is also crucial in assessing the performance of deep learning models for semantic search. This involves examining the model's output on a variety of test queries to ensure that it is returning relevant and meaningful results. By conducting both quantitative and qualitative evaluations, we can gain a comprehensive understanding of the model's strengths and weaknesses.

Finally, deploying the trained model into a production environment is the last step in the process. This involves integrating the model with the existing search infrastructure and ensuring that it can handle real-world search queries efficiently. Techniques such as model compression and optimization are often employed to reduce the model's computational requirements and improve its response time.

To sum it up, training deep learning models for semantic search is a complex yet rewarding endeavor. It requires meticulous data preparation, careful selection of model architecture, effective parameter initialization, rigorous training, and thorough evaluation. By mastering these steps, we can develop robust and accurate semantic search systems that deliver relevant and contextually appropriate search results. The continuous advancements in deep learning and natural language processing promise to further enhance the capabilities of semantic search, paving the way for more sophisticated and intelligent information retrieval systems.

In semantic search, transformer models have become a cornerstone due to their unparalleled ability to understand and process natural language. These models, which have revolutionized the field of natural language processing (NLP), are particularly adept at capturing the intricate nuances of language, making them ideal for semantic search applications. This section will explore the fundamental principles behind transformer models, their unique advantages, and the methodologies for implementing them in semantic search systems.

The advent of transformer models marked a significant departure from traditional neural network architectures. Introduced in the seminal paper "Attention is All You Need" by Vaswani et al., transformers rely on a mechanism known as self-attention to process and encode textual information. Unlike earlier models that processed text sequentially, transformers can analyze entire sentences or documents simultaneously, capturing long-range dependencies and relationships between words. This capability is crucial for semantic search, where understanding the context and meaning of a query is paramount.

At the heart of transformer models lies the self-attention mechanism, which allows the model to weigh the importance of different words in a sentence relative to each other. This is achieved through the computation of attention scores, which determine how much focus should be given to each word when generating the representation of a particular word. By considering the entire context, transformer models can effectively capture the meaning and relationships between words, leading to more accurate and relevant search results.

One of the key innovations of transformer models is the use of multi-head attention. This technique involves running multiple self-attention operations in parallel, each with its set of learned weights. The results of these operations are then concatenated and linearly transformed to produce the final output. Multi-head attention allows the model to capture different aspects of the context simultaneously, enhancing its ability to understand complex language patterns. This is particularly beneficial for semantic search, where queries often contain multiple layers of meaning and nuance.

Another critical component of transformer models is the positional encoding, which provides information about the position of each word in the sequence. Since transformers process text in parallel rather than sequentially, they need a way to incorporate the order of words. Positional encoding achieves this by adding a set of learned or fixed vectors to the input embeddings, ensuring that the model can distinguish between different positions in the text. This positional information is essential for accurately interpreting queries and documents in semantic search.

The training of transformer models for semantic search involves several key steps. First, the model needs to be pre-trained on a large corpus of text to learn general language representations. This pre-training phase typically involves tasks such as masked language modeling, where the model learns to predict missing words in a sentence, and next sentence prediction, where it learns to determine the relationship between consecutive sentences. Pre-training allows the model to acquire a broad understanding of language, which can then be fine-tuned for specific semantic search tasks.

Fine-tuning is the process of adapting a pre-trained transformer model to a particular domain or application. For semantic search, this involves training the model on a dataset of queries and relevant documents. During fine-tuning, the model learns to map queries to relevant results by optimizing for metrics such as relevance and ranking. This phase is crucial for tailoring the model to the specific requirements of semantic search, ensuring that it can deliver accurate and contextually appropriate results.

The implementation of transformer models in semantic search systems also requires careful consideration of the computational resources. Transformers are known for their high computational demands, particularly in terms of memory and processing power. However, recent advancements have led to the development of more efficient variants, such as the DistilBERT and ALBERT models, which reduce the size and complexity of the original transformer architecture while maintaining comparable performance. These lightweight models are more suitable for deployment in real-world semantic search applications, where efficiency and scalability are critical.

One of the most powerful transformer models for semantic search is BERT (Bidirectional Encoder Representations from Transformers), which has set new benchmarks in various NLP tasks. BERT's bidirectional nature allows it to consider both the left and right context of a word simultaneously, leading to a deeper understanding of language. This capability is particularly advantageous for semantic search, where the context of a query can significantly influence the relevance of the results. By leveraging BERT, semantic search systems can achieve a higher level of accuracy and relevance, providing users with more meaningful search experiences.

Another noteworthy transformer model is GPT (Generative Pre-trained Transformer), which excels in generating coherent and contextually appropriate text. While GPT is primarily known for its generative capabilities, it can also be fine-tuned for semantic search tasks. By training GPT on a dataset of queries and relevant documents, it can learn to generate relevant search results based on the input query. This generative approach offers a unique perspective on semantic search, enabling the model to produce diverse and contextually rich results.

The integration of transformer models into semantic search systems also involves the use of specialized libraries and frameworks. Tools such as Hugging Face's Transformers library provide pre-trained models and easy-to-use APIs, simplifying the process of implementing transformer-based semantic search. These libraries offer a wide range of pre-trained models, including BERT, GPT, and their variants, allowing developers to quickly experiment with different architectures and fine-tune them for specific search tasks.

In addition to leveraging pre-trained models, customizing transformer models for semantic search often involves domain-specific adaptations. This can include training the model on specialized corpora, incorporating domain-specific knowledge, and fine-tuning for particular search scenarios. By tailoring the model to the specific requirements of the domain, developers can enhance the relevance and accuracy of the search results, providing users with more targeted and meaningful information.

The evaluation of transformer models in semantic search is a critical aspect of the development process. Traditional evaluation metrics, such as precision, recall, and F1-score, are commonly used to assess the model's performance. However, for semantic search, it is also important to consider more advanced metrics, such as Mean Reciprocal Rank (MRR) and Normalized Discounted Cumulative Gain (NDCG), which provide a comprehensive assessment of the model's ability to rank relevant results. By using these metrics, developers can gain a deeper understanding of the model's strengths and weaknesses, guiding further improvements and optimizations.

In conclusion, transformer models have become an indispensable tool in the development of semantic search systems. Their ability to capture complex language patterns and understand the context of queries makes them ideal for delivering accurate and relevant search results. By leveraging the self-attention mechanism, multi-head attention, and positional encoding, transformer models can process and encode textual information in a way that traditional models cannot. Through careful pre-training, fine-tuning, and evaluation, developers can harness the power of transformer models to create sophisticated and effective semantic search systems. As the field of NLP continues to evolve, transformer models will undoubtedly play a central role in shaping the future of semantic search, enabling more intelligent and context-aware information retrieval.

In the increasingly complex landscape of information retrieval, fine-tuning pre-trained models has emerged as a pivotal strategy for enhancing domain-specific search capabilities. This section delves into the methodologies and best practices for adapting general-purpose models to meet the nuanced demands of specialized domains. By tailoring pre-trained models, we can achieve higher accuracy and relevance in search results, thereby improving user satisfaction and engagement.

The journey of fine-tuning begins with the selection of an appropriate pre-trained model. Numerous models, such as BERT, GPT, and RoBERTa, have demonstrated exceptional performance in natural language understanding tasks. These models provide a robust foundation, having been trained on vast corpora encompassing diverse linguistic patterns. The choice of model depends on various factors, including the complexity of the domain, the type of queries anticipated, and the computational resources available.

Once a suitable model is selected, the first step in fine-tuning involves preparing a domain-specific dataset. This dataset should be representative of the queries and documents typical of the target domain. For instance, a model aimed at legal text searches would benefit from a dataset rich in legal jargon, case laws, and statutes. The quality and relevance of this dataset are paramount, as they directly influence the model's ability to understand and retrieve pertinent information.

The dataset preparation process often involves curating a balanced mix of queries and corresponding relevant documents. Annotating this data for relevance is crucial, as it provides the model with clear guidance on what constitutes a relevant result. Techniques such as manual annotation, crowdsourcing, or leveraging domain experts can be employed to ensure high-quality annotations. Additionally, it is beneficial to include a variety of query types, from simple keyword searches to complex, multi-faceted questions, to train the model comprehensively.

With the dataset in place, the next phase involves adapting the pre-trained model to the domain-specific data. This process, known as fine-tuning, typically employs supervised learning techniques. The model is trained on the annotated dataset, learning to map queries to relevant documents. During this phase, the model's parameters are adjusted to minimize the error between its predictions and the actual annotations. Optimization algorithms, such as Adam or RMSprop, are commonly used to facilitate this process.

One of the critical considerations during fine-tuning is the management of hyperparameters. Hyperparameters, such as learning rate, batch size, and the number of training epochs, play a significant role in the model's performance. Fine-tuning often involves experimenting with different hyperparameter settings to identify the optimal configuration. Techniques like grid search or random search can be employed to systematically explore the hyperparameter space. Additionally, advanced methods, such as Bayesian optimization, offer a more efficient approach to hyperparameter tuning by modeling the performance landscape and guiding the search process.

As the model undergoes fine-tuning, it is essential to monitor its performance continuously. Metrics such as precision, recall, and F1-score provide valuable insights into the model's accuracy and relevance. Moreover, domain-specific metrics, tailored to the particularities of the search tasks, can offer a more nuanced evaluation. For instance, in a medical domain, metrics that account for the clinical significance of retrieved documents might be more informative than generic relevance metrics.

Another vital aspect of fine-tuning is the incorporation of domain-specific knowledge. This can be achieved through various techniques, such as knowledge distillation or transfer learning. Knowledge distillation involves training a smaller, more efficient model (the student) using the predictions of a larger, pre-trained model (the teacher). This approach allows the student model to inherit the teacher's knowledge while being tailored to the specific domain. Transfer learning, on the other hand, leverages pre-trained models as feature extractors, augmenting them with domain-specific layers to enhance their relevance.

In addition to knowledge distillation and transfer learning, integrating domain-specific ontologies and taxonomies can significantly enhance the model's understanding of the domain. Ontologies provide a structured representation of domain concepts and their relationships, enabling the model to capture the hierarchical and semantic nuances of the domain. Incorporating these ontologies into the fine-tuning process can improve the model's ability to recognize and retrieve relevant documents, especially in specialized fields such as biomedical research or legal studies.

Once the fine-tuning process is complete, the model must be rigorously evaluated to ensure its effectiveness in real-world scenarios. This evaluation involves testing the model on a separate, unseen dataset to assess its generalization capabilities. Cross-validation techniques, such as k-fold validation, can provide a comprehensive evaluation by partitioning the dataset into multiple subsets and iteratively training and testing the model on different combinations. This approach helps mitigate the risk of overfitting and ensures that the model performs consistently across various data samples.

Deploying the fine-tuned model into a production environment is the final step in the process. This involves integrating the model with the existing search infrastructure, ensuring that it can handle real-time queries efficiently. Techniques such as model compression and quantization can be employed to optimize the model's performance and reduce its computational footprint. Additionally, implementing a robust monitoring framework is crucial to track the model's performance, identify potential issues, and make necessary adjustments over time.

Conclusively, fine-tuning pre-trained models for domain-specific searches is a multifaceted process that requires careful consideration of various factors, from dataset preparation to hyperparameter tuning and domain-specific adaptations. By leveraging the strengths of pre-trained models and tailoring them to the unique requirements of specialized domains, we can develop highly effective semantic search systems that deliver accurate and relevant results. The continuous advancements in machine learning and natural language processing promise to further enhance the capabilities of fine-tuning, paving the way for more sophisticated and intelligent search solutions in the future.

Evaluating and benchmarking semantic search systems is a crucial phase in the development lifecycle, as it ensures that the system delivers accurate, relevant, and reliable results to end-users. This section delves into the methodologies, metrics, and tools used to assess the performance of semantic search models, offering insights into how these systems can be rigorously tested and optimized for real-world applications.

To begin with, the evaluation of semantic search systems involves a multi-faceted approach, encompassing both quantitative and qualitative assessments. Quantitative evaluation primarily focuses on numerical metrics that quantify the system's performance, while qualitative evaluation involves a more subjective analysis of the search results to ensure they meet user expectations. Balancing these two aspects is vital for a comprehensive understanding of the system's strengths and areas for improvement.

One of the first steps in the evaluation process is the selection of appropriate datasets. These datasets should be representative of the types of queries and documents that the system will encounter in practice. A well-curated evaluation dataset is essential for obtaining meaningful and actionable insights into the system's performance. Typically, these datasets are divided into training, validation, and test sets, with the test set being reserved exclusively for the final evaluation to provide an unbiased assessment.

Quantitative evaluation metrics play a pivotal role in measuring the effectiveness of semantic search systems. Precision, recall, and F1-score are some of the most commonly used metrics. Precision measures the proportion of relevant documents retrieved out of all the documents retrieved, while recall measures the proportion of relevant documents retrieved out of all relevant documents available. The F1-score is the harmonic mean of precision and recall, providing a single metric that balances both aspects. These metrics are particularly useful for understanding the trade-offs between retrieving many documents and ensuring that those documents are relevant.

In addition to precision, recall, and F1-score, other advanced metrics such as Mean Average Precision (MAP) and Normalized Discounted Cumulative Gain (NDCG) are also widely used. MAP calculates the average precision scores for all queries and then takes the mean, providing a comprehensive measure of the system's performance across multiple queries. NDCG, on the other hand, accounts for the position of relevant documents in the search results, with higher relevance scores assigned to documents appearing earlier in the list. This metric is particularly useful for evaluating the ranking effectiveness of semantic search systems.

Another crucial aspect of quantitative evaluation is the use of benchmark datasets and standardized evaluation protocols. Benchmark datasets, such as those provided by the Text Retrieval Conference (TREC) or the Stanford Question Answering Dataset (SQuAD), offer a common ground for comparing the performance of different semantic search systems. These datasets come with predefined queries and relevance judgments, allowing for a consistent and fair comparison. Standardized evaluation protocols ensure that the evaluation process is systematic and reproducible, further enhancing the reliability of the results.

While quantitative metrics provide valuable insights, they do not capture the full picture of a semantic search system's performance. Qualitative evaluation involves a more nuanced analysis of the search results, focusing on aspects such as the relevance, diversity, and user satisfaction. This type of evaluation often involves user studies, where participants interact with the system and provide feedback on the quality of the search results. User studies can reveal important insights that are not apparent from quantitative metrics alone, such as the system's ability to handle ambiguous queries or its responsiveness to user preferences.

Another important tool for qualitative evaluation is the error analysis. By systematically examining the cases where the system fails to retrieve relevant documents or retrieves irrelevant ones, developers can identify patterns and underlying issues that need to be addressed. Error analysis can be particularly useful for uncovering biases in the system, such as a tendency to favor certain types of documents or queries, and for guiding the refinement of the system's algorithms and models.

Benchmarking is another critical component of the evaluation process. Benchmarking involves comparing the performance of the semantic search system against other systems or baselines to gauge its relative effectiveness. This can be done using open-source search engines, commercial systems, or other state-of-the-art models. Benchmarking provides a broader perspective on the system's performance, highlighting its strengths and weaknesses relative to other solutions. It also helps in identifying areas where the system can be improved or optimized.

In addition to traditional benchmarking, the use of challenge competitions and shared tasks has become increasingly popular in the field of semantic search. These competitions, such as those organized by conferences like the Conference on Empirical Methods in Natural

Language Processing (EMNLP) or the Conference on Neural Information Processing Systems (NeurIPS), provide a platform for researchers and practitioners to test their systems against a common set of tasks and datasets. Participating in these competitions can be a valuable way to benchmark the system, gain visibility, and drive innovation.

The tools and frameworks used for evaluation and benchmarking are also an important consideration. Various open-source libraries and platforms, such as the Natural Language Toolkit (NLTK), scikit-learn, and TensorFlow, offer robust support for implementing and evaluating semantic search models. These tools provide a wide range of functionalities, from data preprocessing and feature extraction to model training and evaluation. Leveraging these tools can streamline the evaluation process, making it more efficient and effective.

To sum it up, evaluating and benchmarking semantic search systems is a comprehensive and multi-dimensional process that requires careful consideration of both quantitative and qualitative aspects. By employing a combination of metrics, datasets, user studies, and benchmarking strategies, developers can gain a thorough understanding of their system's performance and identify opportunities for improvement. The continuous evolution of evaluation methodologies and tools promises to further enhance the reliability and effectiveness of semantic search systems, paving the way for more intelligent and user-centric information retrieval solutions.

In the dynamic world of information retrieval, ensuring that semantic search engines operate at peak performance and can scale effectively to handle increasing volumes of data is paramount. As data continues to grow exponentially, search engines must be designed to maintain high-speed query processing and accurate results without compromising on efficiency. This section delves into the strategies and methodologies that can be employed to optimize the performance and scalability of semantic search engines.

One of the fundamental aspects of enhancing the performance of a semantic search engine is optimizing the underlying data structures. Efficient data structures, such as inverted indexes, are crucial for quick lookup and retrieval of documents. Inverted indexes map terms to their locations in the document corpus, allowing for rapid query processing. Additionally, incorporating techniques like term frequency-inverse document frequency (TF-IDF) can further refine the relevance of search results by weighing the importance of terms in the context of the entire corpus.

To further improve performance, caching mechanisms play a vital role. By storing the results of frequently executed queries in memory, caching can significantly reduce the time required to process repeated queries. This is especially useful in scenarios where certain queries are common and executed multiple times. Implementing a multi-level caching strategy, where both query results and intermediate computations are cached, can lead to substantial performance gains. However, it is essential to manage the cache effectively to ensure that it remains up-to-date and does not consume excessive memory resources.

Another critical factor in optimizing performance is the use of parallel processing and distributed computing. Semantic search engines can leverage the power of parallelism to process multiple queries or parts of a query simultaneously. This can be achieved through multi-threading or by distributing the workload across multiple machines in a cluster. Distributed computing frameworks, such as Apache Hadoop and Apache Spark, provide robust solutions for handling large-scale data processing tasks. By distributing the data and computation across a cluster of machines, these frameworks enable search engines to scale horizontally and handle massive datasets efficiently.

Load balancing is also an essential component of a scalable semantic search engine. As the volume of queries increases, it is crucial to distribute the workload evenly across the available resources to prevent any single machine from becoming a bottleneck. Load balancers can dynamically allocate incoming queries to the least loaded servers, ensuring optimal utilization of resources and maintaining high throughput. Additionally, techniques like query routing and sharding can be employed to divide the data and queries into smaller, manageable chunks, further enhancing scalability.

In addition to optimizing the search engine's architecture, fine-tuning the search algorithms is crucial for improving performance. Techniques such as query expansion and relevance feedback can enhance the accuracy of search results by incorporating user interactions and contextual information. Query expansion involves augmenting the original query with additional terms that are semantically related, thereby increasing the chances of retrieving relevant documents. Relevance feedback, on the other hand, utilizes user feedback to refine the search results iteratively, improving their precision and recall over time.

Machine learning models also play a significant role in optimizing semantic search engines. By training models on historical query data and user interactions, search engines can learn to predict and rank relevant documents more effectively. Techniques such as learning to rank (LTR) can be employed to train models that optimize the ordering of search results based on various relevance signals. Additionally, incorporating deep learning models, such as convolutional neural networks (CNNs) and recurrent neural networks (RNNs), can further enhance the semantic understanding of queries and documents, leading to more accurate and contextually relevant search results.

Another important aspect of optimizing performance is the efficient handling of large-scale data. As the volume of data grows, it becomes increasingly challenging to store, manage, and retrieve information efficiently. Employing data compression techniques can help reduce the storage requirements and improve the speed of data transfer. Techniques such as delta encoding, run-length encoding, and Huffman coding can be used to compress the data without significant loss of information. Additionally, indexing strategies like B-trees and KD-trees can be employed to organize the data in a way that allows for fast and efficient retrieval.

Monitoring and profiling are essential practices for maintaining the performance of a semantic search engine. By continuously monitoring the system's performance metrics, such as query latency, throughput, and resource utilization, potential bottlenecks and performance issues can be identified and addressed proactively. Profiling tools can provide detailed insights into the system's behavior, allowing developers to pinpoint the root causes of performance degradation and optimize the relevant components. Regular performance audits and stress testing can ensure that the search engine remains robust and responsive under varying load conditions.

Scalability also involves ensuring that the search engine can handle a growing number of users and queries without compromising on performance. One approach to achieving this is through the use of cloud-based infrastructure. Cloud platforms, such as Amazon Web Services (AWS), Google Cloud Platform (GCP), and Microsoft Azure, offer scalable and flexible solutions for deploying and managing semantic search engines. By leveraging cloud services, search engines can dynamically scale their resources based on demand, ensuring high availability and performance. Additionally, cloud-based solutions provide built-in redundancy and failover mechanisms, enhancing the reliability and resilience of the search engine.

To conclude, optimizing the performance and scalability of semantic search engines requires a multifaceted approach that encompasses efficient data structures, caching mechanisms, parallel processing, load balancing, algorithm fine-tuning, machine learning, data compression, and continuous monitoring. By employing these strategies, search engines can deliver fast, accurate, and relevant results to users, even as the volume of data and queries continues to grow. The ongoing advancements in technology and computing infrastructure promise to further enhance the capabilities of semantic search engines, enabling them to meet the ever-evolving demands of information retrieval in the digital age.

Enhancing Search Results With Entity Recognition And Linking

Introduction to Entity Recognition and Linking

Semantic search has revolutionized the way we retrieve information by understanding the context and meaning behind user queries. A crucial aspect of this advanced search methodology is entity recognition and linking, which significantly enhances the precision and relevance of search results. This section delves into the foundational principles of these techniques, their importance in semantic search, and how they work together to improve the search experience.

Entity recognition, also known as named entity recognition (NER), is the process of identifying and classifying entities inside a text. These entities can be names of people, organizations, locations, dates, and other specific items that provide context to the content. For instance, in the sentence "Apple announced the new iPhone in California," NER would identify "Apple" as an organization, "iPhone" as a product, and "California" as a location. By recognizing these entities, search systems can better understand the user's intent and provide more accurate results.

There are several approaches to entity recognition, ranging from rule-based methods to machine learning techniques. Rule-based methods rely on predefined patterns and dictionaries to identify entities. While these methods can be effective, they often lack the flexibility to handle the nuances and variations in natural language. On the other hand, machine learning approaches, particularly those utilizing deep learning, have shown remarkable success in NER tasks. These models learn from large datasets and can generalize better to unseen data, making them more robust and accurate.

Once entities are recognized, the next step is entity linking, which involves associating these entities with their corresponding entries in a knowledge base. This process is also known as entity disambiguation. For example, the word "Apple" could refer to the fruit or the technology company, depending on the context. Entity linking resolves such ambiguities by linking the recognized entity to the appropriate entry in a knowledge base like Wikipedia or a domain-specific database. This step is crucial for providing meaningful and contextually relevant search results.

Entity linking typically involves two main components: candidate generation and candidate ranking. In candidate generation, potential matches for the recognized entity are retrieved from the knowledge base. For instance, if the entity is "Paris," the system might generate candidates such as Paris, France, and Paris, Texas. In the candidate ranking phase, these potential matches are evaluated based on various features, such as contextual similarity and prior probabilities, to determine the best match. Advanced machine learning models, including those based on neural networks, are often employed to improve the accuracy of this ranking process.

The synergy between entity recognition and linking plays a pivotal role in enhancing search results. By accurately identifying and disambiguating entities, search systems can understand the context of user queries more effectively. This leads to more precise retrieval of information, as the system can filter out irrelevant results and focus on the most pertinent ones. For example, a query like "latest news on Amazon" would yield results related to the company Amazon rather than the Amazon rainforest, thanks to effective entity recognition and linking.

Moreover, these techniques enable the enrichment of search results with additional information. By linking entities to a comprehensive knowledge base, search engines can provide users with a richer and more informative experience. For instance, a search for "Barack Obama" might not only return news articles but also display a knowledge panel with biographical information, recent activities, and related entities. This multidimensional approach to search results enhances user satisfaction and engagement.

Implementing entity recognition and linking in search systems involves several technical challenges. One of the primary challenges is ensuring the scalability and efficiency of these processes, especially when dealing with large volumes of data. Advanced indexing techniques, parallel processing, and optimization algorithms are often employed to address these issues. Additionally, maintaining the accuracy and relevance of the knowledge base is critical, as outdated or incorrect information can lead to erroneous search results.

Another challenge is handling the diversity and complexity of natural language. Entities can appear in various forms, including abbreviations, synonyms, and misspellings. Robust NER and linking models must be capable of handling these variations to ensure accurate identification and disambiguation. Continuous learning and adaptation are essential, as language evolves and new entities emerge over time.

In summary, entity recognition and linking are fundamental components of semantic search that significantly enhance the quality of search results. By identifying and disambiguating

95

entities, these techniques enable search systems to understand user queries more deeply and provide more relevant and informative responses. As the field of natural language processing continues to advance, we can expect even more sophisticated and effective methods for entity recognition and linking, further improving the search experience for users.

Entity extraction is a cornerstone of semantic search, serving as the gateway for transforming raw text into structured data that can be more easily interpreted and utilized by search systems. This section delves into various methodologies for extracting entities from text, outlining their strengths, limitations, and practical applications. The goal is to provide a comprehensive understanding of the techniques available for entity extraction, equipping readers with the knowledge to choose and implement the most suitable approach for their specific needs.

One of the earliest and most straightforward methods for entity extraction is the use of rule-based systems. These systems rely on predefined rules and patterns to identify entities inside a text. For example, a rule might specify that any capitalized word following a title like "Dr." or "Mr." is likely a person's name. Similarly, specific patterns can be used to identify dates, addresses, or other types of entities. Rule-based systems are relatively easy to implement and can be highly effective in controlled environments where the text follows predictable patterns. However, they often struggle with the variability and ambiguity inherent in natural language, making them less suitable for more complex or diverse datasets.

To address the limitations of rule-based systems, statistical methods for entity extraction have been developed. These approaches leverage probabilistic models to identify entities based on the likelihood of certain words or phrases appearing in specific contexts. One common statistical method is the use of Hidden Markov Models (HMMs), which treat entity extraction as a sequence labeling problem. In this framework, each word in a sentence is assigned a label indicating whether it is part of an entity and, if so, what type of entity it is. HMMs can capture the dependencies between words and their labels, allowing for more accurate entity extraction compared to simple rule-based systems. Nonetheless, they still require a significant amount of labeled training data and may struggle with long-range dependencies in text.

Machine learning techniques have further advanced the field of entity extraction, with supervised learning algorithms playing a pivotal role. In supervised learning, models are trained on annotated datasets where entities are explicitly labeled. Popular algorithms for entity extraction include Conditional Random Fields (CRFs) and Support Vector Machines (SVMs). CRFs, in particular, have gained widespread adoption due to their ability to model the relationships between neighboring words and labels, resulting in more accurate and context-aware entity extraction. However, the performance of supervised learning models is heavily dependent on the quality and quantity of the training data, and creating large annotated datasets can be a labor-intensive process.

The advent of deep learning has revolutionized entity extraction, offering powerful new techniques that surpass traditional methods in terms of accuracy and flexibility. Recurrent Neural Networks (RNNs), and their more advanced variants like Long Short-Term Memory (LSTM) networks and Gated Recurrent Units (GRUs), have shown remarkable success in sequence labeling tasks, including entity extraction. These models are capable of capturing long-range dependencies and complex patterns in text, making them well-suited for handling the nuances of natural language. Furthermore, the introduction of transformer-based models, such as BERT (Bidirectional Encoder Representations from Transformers), has set new benchmarks in entity extraction performance. These models leverage self-attention mechanisms to process entire sentences at once, capturing intricate relationships between words and enabling highly accurate entity extraction.

In addition to these supervised approaches, unsupervised and semi-supervised methods have also emerged as viable options for entity extraction. Unsupervised methods, such as clustering and topic modeling, do not require labeled training data and instead rely on the inherent structure of the text to identify entities. For example, clustering algorithms can group similar words or phrases together, potentially revealing entities based on their co-occurrence patterns. Topic modeling techniques, like Latent Dirichlet Allocation (LDA), can uncover hidden topics inside a corpus, which may correspond to specific entities. While unsupervised methods are less accurate than supervised approaches, they offer the advantage of being able to operate on unlabeled data, making them useful in scenarios where labeled datasets are scarce.

Semi-supervised techniques combine elements of both supervised and unsupervised learning, aiming to leverage the strengths of each. One common approach is to use a small labeled dataset to train an initial model, which is then used to annotate a larger unlabeled dataset. The newly labeled data can be used to retrain the model, iteratively improving its performance. This process, known as self-training or bootstrapping, can help mitigate the challenges associated with obtaining large annotated datasets. Another semi-supervised method is co-training, where multiple models are trained on different views of the data and collaboratively improve each other by sharing their predictions. These techniques can enhance entity extraction performance while reducing the reliance on extensive labeled data.

Regardless of the specific technique employed, there are several key considerations that influence the effectiveness of entity extraction. One crucial factor is the quality of the text preprocessing pipeline. Preprocessing steps, such as tokenization, stemming, and lemmatization, play a vital role in preparing the text for entity extraction. Properly handling punctuation, capitalization, and other textual nuances can significantly impact the accuracy of the extracted entities. Additionally, the choice of features used to represent the text is critical. Features can range from simple lexical attributes, like word counts and part-of-speech tags, to more sophisticated representations, such as word embeddings and contextualized vectors. Selecting the appropriate features for the specific entity extraction task can greatly influence the model's performance.

Another important consideration is the domain-specific nature of entity extraction. Different domains may require tailored approaches to effectively identify and classify entities. For instance, medical texts may contain specialized terminology and abbreviations that necessitate domain-specific models and dictionaries. Similarly, legal documents may require custom rules and patterns to accurately extract entities like case names and statutes. Adapting entity extraction techniques to the specific characteristics and requirements of the target domain is essential for achieving optimal results.

In essence, the landscape of entity extraction is rich and varied, encompassing a wide range of techniques from rule-based systems to advanced deep learning models. Each approach has its own strengths and limitations, and the choice of technique depends on factors such as the complexity of the text, the availability of labeled data, and the specific requirements of the application. By understanding the different methodologies and their practical

100

implications, practitioners can make informed decisions and implement effective entity extraction solutions that enhance the performance of semantic search systems.

In the evolving landscape of information retrieval, linking entities to knowledge bases has emerged as a vital technique for refining search outcomes. By bridging the gap between raw data and structured knowledge, this process enhances the ability of search systems to comprehend and respond to user queries with greater precision and relevance. This section delves into the intricacies of entity linking, exploring its methodologies, challenges, and the significant impact it has on the effectiveness of semantic search.

Entity linking, at its core, involves associating identified entities inside a text to their corresponding entries in a structured knowledge repository. This task is pivotal in disambiguating entities, ensuring that the search system accurately interprets and matches user queries to the correct information. For instance, consider a user searching for "Tesla." Without entity linking, the system might return results related to Nikola Tesla, the inventor, or Tesla, the car manufacturer. By linking the entity to a knowledge base, the system can discern the context and provide results pertinent to the user's intent.

The process of linking entities begins with entity recognition, where the system identifies potential entities inside the text. These entities can range from names of individuals and organizations to dates and specific terms. Once recognized, the next step involves generating candidate entities from the knowledge base. This candidate generation phase is crucial as it lays the groundwork for accurate linking. For example, if the recognized entity is "Washington," the system might generate candidates such as George Washington, Washington D.C., and the state of Washington.

Following candidate generation, the system must rank these candidates to determine the most appropriate match. This ranking process involves evaluating various features, such as contextual similarity, entity popularity, and prior probabilities. Contextual similarity assesses how closely the surrounding text matches the context of the candidate entities. Entity popularity can be a useful feature, as more prominent entities are often more likely to be the correct match. Prior probabilities, derived from historical data or domain-specific knowledge, provide additional guidance in ranking the candidates.

Machine learning models play a significant role in enhancing the accuracy of entity linking. These models are trained on large datasets containing annotated examples of entity links, enabling them to learn patterns and relationships that inform the ranking process. Advanced models, including those based on neural networks, have demonstrated remarkable success in this domain. By leveraging deep learning techniques, these models can capture intricate dependencies and nuances in the text, leading to more precise and reliable entity linking.

One of the primary challenges in entity linking is managing the ambiguity and variability inherent in natural language. Entities can have multiple forms, such as abbreviations, synonyms, and misspellings, making it difficult to consistently identify and link them. For instance, the entity "IBM" might appear as "International Business Machines" or simply "I.B.M." Robust entity linking systems must be capable of handling these variations to ensure accurate results. Continuous learning and adaptation are essential, as language evolves and new entities emerge over time.

Another challenge lies in maintaining the scalability and efficiency of the entity linking process, especially when dealing with extensive datasets. Large-scale search systems must be able to process vast amounts of data quickly and accurately. This necessitates the use of advanced indexing techniques, parallel processing, and optimization algorithms. These methods help ensure that the entity linking process remains efficient and responsive, even under heavy loads.

The quality and comprehensiveness of the knowledge base also play a crucial role in the success of entity linking. A well-maintained knowledge base provides a rich source of information that enhances the system's ability to accurately link entities. However, outdated or incomplete knowledge bases can lead to erroneous links and reduce the overall effectiveness of the search system. Regular updates and validation of the knowledge base are essential to maintain its accuracy and relevance.

The impact of effective entity linking on search results is profound. By accurately linking entities to a structured knowledge base, search systems can deliver more relevant and informative responses to user queries. This not only improves the precision of search results but also enriches the user experience by providing additional context and information. For example, a search for "Albert Einstein" might return not only biographical details but also related concepts, such as his contributions to the theory of relativity and his influence on modern physics.

Moreover, entity linking enables the integration of diverse data sources, creating a more holistic view of the information. By linking entities across various domains, search systems can provide users with a comprehensive understanding of complex topics. This multidimensional approach to information retrieval fosters deeper engagement and facilitates more informed decision-making.

To conclude, linking entities to knowledge bases is a fundamental component of semantic search that significantly enhances the quality and relevance of search results. Through sophisticated methodologies and advanced machine learning techniques, entity linking disambiguates entities and connects them to structured knowledge, enabling search systems to better understand and respond to user queries. As the field of natural language processing continues to evolve, we can anticipate even more refined and effective approaches to entity linking, further improving the search experience for users.

In search technologies, enhancing the precision of search outcomes is of paramount importance. One innovative method that has shown significant promise is entity contextualization. This technique goes beyond merely identifying entities inside a text by delving into the deeper understanding of the context in which these entities are situated. By effectively contextualizing entities, search systems can provide more accurate and relevant results, thereby greatly improving the user experience.

Entity contextualization involves a comprehensive analysis of the surrounding text to discern the specific meaning and relevance of an entity inside a given context. For instance, consider a search query that includes the term "Mercury." Without contextualization, the search system might struggle to determine whether the user is referring to the planet, the chemical element, or the Roman god. By analyzing the surrounding words and phrases, the system can infer the intended meaning and deliver more pertinent results.

One of the foundational techniques in entity contextualization is the use of co-occurrence patterns. This approach examines the frequency and proximity of words that appear alongside the entity in question. For instance, if the term "Mercury" frequently appears near words like "planet," "solar system," or "orbit," the system can infer that the entity likely refers to the celestial body. Conversely, if "Mercury" is found near terms like "thermometer," "poisoning," or "Hg," it is more likely referring to the element. By leveraging these patterns, search systems can more accurately interpret the context of entities and refine their results accordingly.

Another critical aspect of entity contextualization is the integration of domain-specific knowledge. Different fields of knowledge have unique terminologies and contextual cues that can significantly impact the interpretation of entities. For example, in the medical domain, the term "jaguar" might refer to a specific model of a medical device, whereas in the automotive industry, it would likely refer to the car brand. By incorporating domain-specific knowledge bases and ontologies, search systems can better understand and contextualize entities inside specialized fields, leading to more precise search outcomes.

Machine learning models have also played a pivotal role in advancing entity contextualization. These models are trained on vast amounts of annotated data, allowing them to learn complex relationships and dependencies between words and entities. Techniques such as word embeddings, which represent words in continuous vector spaces, enable models to capture semantic similarities and contextual nuances. For instance, word embeddings can help a search system understand that "Jaguar" in the context of "car" is more similar to "BMW" or "Mercedes" than to "cheetah" or "leopard." This deeper understanding of context allows for more accurate disambiguation and relevance ranking.

Contextualization can be further enhanced by incorporating temporal and spatial information. Entities often have different meanings depending on the time or location in which they are mentioned. For instance, the term "Olympics" could refer to the Summer or Winter Games, and its context might change depending on the year or city being discussed. By integrating temporal and spatial data, search systems can better understand the specific context of entities and deliver results that are more aligned with the user's intent.

Moreover, the use of conversational context is becoming increasingly important in modern search systems, particularly with the rise of voice-activated assistants and chatbots. In a conversation, the meaning of entities can evolve based on the preceding dialogue. For example, in a dialogue where a user first asks about "Mercury" and then follows up with a question about "its atmosphere," the system can infer that the user is referring to the planet Mercury. By maintaining and analyzing the conversational context, search systems can provide more coherent and contextually appropriate responses.

The integration of user-specific context also plays a crucial role in entity contextualization. Personalization techniques can leverage information about a user's search history, preferences, and behavior to tailor search results more effectively. For instance, if a user frequently searches for information related to astronomy, the term "Mercury" in their queries is more likely to refer to the planet rather than the element. By incorporating user-specific context, search systems can deliver results that are more relevant to the individual user, enhancing their overall search experience.

Implementing entity contextualization in search systems presents several technical challenges. One of the primary challenges is ensuring the scalability and efficiency of the contextualization process, particularly when dealing with large volumes of data. Advanced indexing techniques, parallel processing, and optimization algorithms are often employed to address these issues. Additionally, maintaining the accuracy and relevance of the contextual information is critical, as outdated or incorrect context can lead to erroneous search results.

Another challenge is handling the diversity and complexity of natural language. Contextual cues can vary widely across different languages, dialects, and cultural contexts. Robust entity contextualization models must be capable of handling these variations to ensure accurate interpretation and disambiguation. Continuous learning and adaptation are essential, as language evolves and new contextual patterns emerge over time.

In conclusion, entity contextualization is a powerful technique for improving the accuracy and relevance of search results. By analyzing the surrounding text, integrating domain-specific knowledge, leveraging machine learning models, and incorporating temporal, spatial, conversational, and user-specific context, search systems can better understand the meaning and relevance of entities. This deeper understanding enables more precise disambiguation and relevance ranking, leading to a more satisfying and effective search experience for users. As the field of natural language processing continues to advance, we can expect even more sophisticated and effective methods for entity contextualization, further enhancing the capabilities of search systems.

In the ever-evolving landscape of information retrieval, one of the most challenging aspects is managing the ambiguity inherent in natural language. When users input queries, the search system must not only recognize the entities mentioned but also accurately disambiguate them to provide relevant results. This section delves into the complexities of handling ambiguity in entity recognition and linking, exploring various strategies and methodologies to enhance the precision and relevance of search outcomes.

Natural language is fraught with ambiguities, where the same word or phrase can have multiple meanings depending on context. For instance, consider the word "jaguar." It could refer to the animal, a car brand, or even a sports team. Without proper disambiguation, a search system might return irrelevant results, leading to a poor user experience. Therefore, addressing ambiguity is crucial for the effectiveness of entity recognition and linking.

One of the primary strategies for disambiguation involves contextual analysis. By examining the words and phrases surrounding an ambiguous entity, the system can infer its intended meaning. For example, if the term "jaguar" appears alongside words like "zoo," "wildlife," or "predator," it is likely referring to the animal. On the other hand, if it is found near terms like "luxury," "sedan," or "car dealership," the system can deduce that the entity refers to the car brand. Contextual clues play a pivotal role in narrowing down the possible meanings of an entity, thereby enhancing the accuracy of the search results.

Another effective approach is leveraging external knowledge bases. These repositories contain vast amounts of structured information about various entities, including their attributes, relationships, and contexts. By linking recognized entities to entries in a knowledge base, the system can utilize this structured information to resolve ambiguities. For instance, if the entity "apple" is linked to a knowledge base entry that includes attributes like "fruit" or "technology company," the system can use this information to disambiguate the term based on the query context. Knowledge bases act as valuable resources for enriching the entity recognition and linking process, providing additional layers of information that aid in disambiguation.

Machine learning models have significantly advanced the field of entity disambiguation. These models are trained on large datasets containing annotated examples of ambiguous entities and their correct interpretations. By learning patterns and relationships from these examples, machine learning models can predict the most likely meaning of an ambiguous entity in a given context. Advanced models, such as those based on neural networks, have demonstrated remarkable success in this domain. They can capture intricate dependencies and nuances in the text, leading to more precise disambiguation. For instance, a neural network model might learn that the term "jaguar" is more likely to refer to the animal in a wildlife conservation article, whereas it is more likely to refer to the car brand in an automotive review.

Incorporating user-specific information is another powerful strategy for handling ambiguity. Personalization techniques leverage data about a user's search history, preferences, and behavior to tailor search results more effectively. For example, if a user frequently searches for information related to technology, the term "apple" in their queries is more likely to refer to the technology company rather than the fruit. By utilizing user-specific context, search systems can provide results that are more relevant to the individual's interests, thereby reducing ambiguity and enhancing the overall search experience.

Temporal and spatial information can also play a crucial role in disambiguation. Entities often have different meanings depending on the time or location in which they are mentioned. For instance, the term "election" could refer to different events depending on the year or country being discussed. By integrating temporal and spatial data, search systems can better understand the specific context of entities and deliver results that are more aligned with the user's intent. For example, if a user queries "election results," the system can use the current date and the user's location to infer which election they are referring to and provide the most relevant information.

Conversational context is becoming increasingly important in modern search systems, particularly with the rise of voice-activated assistants and chatbots. In a conversation, the meaning of entities can evolve based on the preceding dialogue. For instance, if a user first asks about "Mercury" and then follows up with a question about "its atmosphere," the system can infer that the user is referring to the planet Mercury. By maintaining and analyzing the conversational context, search systems can provide more coherent and contextually appropriate responses, thereby reducing ambiguity.

Despite these advancements, several challenges remain in handling ambiguity in entity recognition and linking. One of the primary challenges is ensuring the scalability and efficiency of the disambiguation process, particularly when dealing with large volumes of data. Advanced indexing techniques, parallel processing, and optimization algorithms are often employed to address these issues. Additionally, maintaining the accuracy and relevance of the contextual information is critical, as outdated or incorrect context can lead to erroneous search results.

Another challenge is the diversity and complexity of natural language. Contextual cues can vary widely across different languages, dialects, and cultural contexts. Robust disambiguation models must be capable of handling these variations to ensure accurate interpretation and linking of entities. Continuous learning and adaptation are essential, as language evolves and new contextual patterns emerge over time. For instance, the term "cloud" might have different meanings in meteorology and technology, and new interpretations might arise as these fields evolve.

In summary, handling ambiguity in entity recognition and linking is a multifaceted challenge that requires a combination of contextual analysis, external knowledge bases, machine learning models, and user-specific information. By leveraging these strategies, search systems can more accurately interpret ambiguous entities and provide relevant results, thereby enhancing the overall search experience. As the field of natural language processing continues to advance, we can expect even more sophisticated and effective methods for disambiguation, further improving the capabilities of search systems.

In modern search technologies, the integration of entity recognition into search pipelines is a transformative approach that significantly enhances the precision and relevance of search results. Entity recognition, the process of identifying and classifying key elements inside a text, such as names of people, places, organizations, dates, and other specific terms, allows search systems to understand and interpret user queries with a higher degree of accuracy. This section explores the methodologies and strategies for incorporating entity recognition into search pipelines, highlighting its impact on search performance and user experience.

To begin with, the integration of entity recognition into search pipelines involves several key steps. The initial phase is the preprocessing of the input text. Preprocessing includes tasks such as tokenization, where the text is broken down into individual words or tokens, and normalization, which involves converting text into a standard format. This may include lowercasing, removing special characters, and handling various forms of punctuation. These preprocessing steps are crucial as they prepare the text for the subsequent entity recognition process.

Once the text is preprocessed, the next step is the actual entity recognition. This involves using machine learning models and natural language processing (NLP) techniques to identify and classify entities inside the text. Various approaches can be employed for entity recognition, including rule-based systems, statistical models, and deep learning techniques. Rule-based systems use predefined patterns and heuristics to identify entities, while statistical models leverage probabilistic methods to make predictions based on training data. Deep learning techniques, such as recurrent neural networks (RNNs) and transformer models, have shown remarkable success in accurately recognizing entities by learning complex patterns and dependencies inside the text.

A critical component of entity recognition is the use of labeled training data. Training data consists of text annotated with entity labels, which the machine learning models use to learn how to identify and classify entities. The quality and quantity of training data play a significant role in the performance of the entity recognition system. High-quality, diverse datasets that cover various domains and contexts enable the models to generalize better and achieve higher accuracy. Additionally, continuous learning and updating of the models with new data help maintain their effectiveness as language and usage patterns evolve.

After entities are recognized inside the text, the next step in the search pipeline is to incorporate this information into the indexing process. Indexing involves creating a structured representation of the text that allows for efficient retrieval of information. By including recognized entities in the index, the search system can perform more sophisticated queries and provide more relevant results. For example, if a user searches for information about a specific person, the system can prioritize documents that mention the recognized entity corresponding to that person. This enhances the precision of search results by ensuring that the most relevant documents are retrieved.

In addition to improving the indexing process, integrating entity recognition into search pipelines also enhances the ranking of search results. Ranking algorithms determine the order in which search results are presented to the user, based on their relevance to the query. By incorporating entity information into the ranking process, search systems can better assess the relevance of documents. For instance, documents that contain recognized entities matching the query can be given higher priority, as they are more likely to be relevant to the user's intent. This leads to a more satisfying search experience, as users receive results that are more closely aligned with their queries.

Furthermore, entity recognition enables the implementation of advanced search features, such as faceted search and semantic search. Faceted search allows users to refine their search results by applying filters based on recognized entities. For example, in an e-commerce search system, users can filter results by brand, category, or price range, based on the recognized entities associated with the products. Semantic search goes a step further by understanding the meaning and context of the query, rather than relying solely on keyword matching. By leveraging entity recognition, semantic search systems can comprehend the user's intent and provide more accurate and contextually relevant results.

Another significant advantage of integrating entity recognition into search pipelines is the ability to handle complex and ambiguous queries more effectively. Natural language is inherently ambiguous, and the same word or phrase can have multiple meanings depending on the context. Entity recognition helps disambiguate these terms by identifying the specific entities mentioned in the query. For example, if a user searches for "Paris," the system can recognize whether the query refers to Paris, France, or Paris, Texas, based on the surrounding context and the recognized entities. This disambiguation process ensures that users receive results that are pertinent to their intended meaning.

The integration of entity recognition into search pipelines also facilitates the extraction of structured information from unstructured text. Unstructured text, such as articles, blog posts, and social media content, often contains valuable information that is not readily accessible through traditional keyword-based search methods. By recognizing and extracting entities from unstructured text, search systems can create structured representations of the information, making it easier to retrieve and analyze. For example, a search system can extract entities such as names, dates, and locations from a news article, allowing users to perform more targeted searches and obtain specific information.

Implementing entity recognition in search pipelines presents several technical challenges. One of the primary challenges is ensuring the scalability and efficiency of the entity recognition process, particularly when dealing with large volumes of data. Advanced indexing techniques, parallel processing, and optimization algorithms are often employed to address these issues. Additionally, maintaining the accuracy and relevance of the recognized entities is critical, as outdated or incorrect entity information can lead to erroneous search results. Continuous monitoring and updating of the entity recognition models and training data are essential to ensure their effectiveness.

Another challenge is handling the diversity and complexity of natural language. Entity recognition models must be capable of recognizing entities across different languages, dialects, and domains. This requires extensive training data and sophisticated modeling techniques to capture the nuances and variations in language. Additionally, entity recognition systems must be able to handle various forms of entity mentions, such as abbreviations, acronyms, and misspellings. Robust models that can generalize across different contexts and handle these variations are crucial for accurate entity recognition.

To conclude, integrating entity recognition into search pipelines is a powerful approach that significantly enhances the precision and relevance of search results. By identifying and classifying key elements inside the text, search systems can better understand and interpret user queries, leading to more accurate and contextually relevant results. The incorporation of entity recognition into the indexing and ranking processes, as well as the implementation of advanced search features, further improves the search experience for users. Despite the technical challenges, the benefits of entity recognition in search pipelines are substantial, making it a valuable component of modern search technologies. As the field of natural language processing continues to advance, we can expect even more sophisticated and effective methods for integrating entity recognition into search pipelines, further enhancing the capabilities of search systems.

In the ever-evolving landscape of information retrieval, the implementation of entity linking has proven to be a game-changer in enhancing search results. By linking identified entities in text to structured data sources, search systems can provide users with more accurate and contextually relevant information. This section delves into various case studies that illustrate how entity linking has been successfully applied to improve search outcomes across different domains.

One of the most notable examples of entity linking in action is in the field of academic research. Researchers often need to sift through vast amounts of literature to find relevant studies, papers, and articles. Traditional keyword-based search systems can be inadequate, as they may return results that are only tangentially related to the query. By incorporating entity linking, academic search engines can disambiguate terms and link them to specific authors, institutions, or research topics. For instance, a search for "machine learning" can be linked to renowned researchers in the field, their seminal papers, and affiliated institutions. This not only narrows down the search results to the most pertinent documents but also provides a richer context, aiding researchers in their quest for knowledge.

In e-commerce, entity linking has been instrumental in enhancing product search capabilities. Online shoppers often use ambiguous or colloquial terms to describe the products they are looking for. Traditional search systems might struggle to interpret these queries accurately, leading to irrelevant or incomplete results. By implementing entity linking, e-commerce platforms can map user queries to specific product attributes, brands, or categories. For example, a search for "Nike running shoes" can be linked to the brand

"Nike," the product category "running shoes," and specific product models. This ensures that the search results are highly relevant to the user's intent, thereby improving the shopping experience and increasing the likelihood of purchase.

The healthcare industry has also benefited significantly from the application of entity linking in search systems. Medical professionals often need to access a wide range of information, from clinical guidelines and research articles to patient records and drug databases. Entity linking enables these search systems to accurately interpret medical terminology and link it to relevant entities, such as diseases, treatments, and medications. For instance, a search for "diabetes management" can be linked to clinical guidelines on diabetes care, research articles on the latest treatment options, and patient education materials. This comprehensive approach ensures that healthcare providers have access to the most relevant and up-to-date information, ultimately improving patient care.

In the domain of news and media, entity linking has revolutionized the way users consume information. News articles often contain references to people, places, events, and organizations that may not be immediately recognizable to all readers. By linking these entities to structured data sources, news platforms can provide additional context and background information. For example, an article about a political event can link the names of politicians to their biographies, previous news coverage, and related events. This not only enhances the reader's understanding of the article but also encourages deeper engagement with the content. Moreover, entity linking can help news platforms identify and group related articles, providing users with a more cohesive and comprehensive news experience.

In the financial sector, entity linking has been utilized to improve the accuracy and relevance of search results in financial databases and news services. Financial professionals often need to track information about companies, stocks, and market trends. Traditional search systems might return a plethora of unrelated results, making it difficult to find the most pertinent information. By implementing entity linking, financial search systems can map queries to specific companies, stock symbols, and financial terms. For instance, a search for "Apple Inc. quarterly earnings" can be linked to the company's financial reports, stock performance data, and related news articles. This ensures that financial professionals have quick and easy access to the most relevant information, enabling them to make informed decisions.

The travel industry has also seen significant improvements in search capabilities through the use of entity linking. Travelers often use vague or broad terms when searching for travel information, such as "beach vacation" or "European tour." Traditional search systems might struggle to interpret these queries and return a mix of unrelated results. By incorporating entity linking, travel search engines can map user queries to specific destinations, travel packages, and activities. For example, a search for "beach vacation" can be linked to popular beach destinations, resort options, and travel itineraries. This ensures that travelers receive highly relevant and targeted information, making it easier for them to plan their trips.

In the field of legal research, entity linking has been employed to enhance the search capabilities of legal databases. Legal professionals often need to find case laws, statutes, and legal opinions that are relevant to their cases. Traditional keyword-based search systems might return a multitude of unrelated documents, making it challenging to find the most pertinent information. By implementing entity linking, legal search systems can map queries to specific legal entities, such as cases, statutes, and judicial opinions. For instance, a search for "contract law" can be linked to landmark cases, relevant statutes, and legal commentaries. This ensures that legal professionals have access to the most relevant and authoritative information, aiding them in their legal research and case preparation.

In the context of customer support, entity linking has been leveraged to improve the search capabilities of knowledge bases and help centers. Customers often use natural language queries to find solutions to their problems, which can be challenging for traditional search systems to interpret accurately. By incorporating entity linking, customer support search systems can map queries to specific products, issues, and solutions. For example, a search for "troubleshooting iPhone battery issues" can be linked to relevant help articles, troubleshooting guides, and user forums. This ensures that customers receive accurate and relevant information, improving their support experience and reducing the need for human intervention.

In essence, the implementation of entity linking has significantly enhanced search results across various domains, from academic research and e-commerce to healthcare and news media. By linking identified entities to structured data sources, search systems can provide users with more accurate, contextually relevant, and comprehensive information. The case studies presented in this section illustrate the transformative impact of entity linking on search capabilities, highlighting its potential to improve user experience and drive better outcomes in diverse fields. As technology continues to advance, we can expect even more sophisticated applications of entity linking, further enhancing the capabilities of search systems and the quality of information retrieval.

Evaluating And Optimizing Semantic Search Systems

Metrics for Evaluating Semantic Search Systems

Evaluating the performance of semantic search systems is crucial to ensuring that they deliver relevant and accurate results to users. This section delves into the various metrics that can be employed to assess the effectiveness of these systems. By understanding and measuring these metrics, developers and researchers can fine-tune their algorithms and improve the overall search experience.

One of the foundational metrics used in evaluating semantic search systems is precision. Precision measures the proportion of relevant results returned out of the total results retrieved. For instance, if a search query retrieves ten documents, and six of them are relevant to the query, the precision is 0.6 or 60%. High precision indicates that the system is effective at filtering out irrelevant content and presenting the user with pertinent information.

Another critical metric is recall, which assesses the system's ability to retrieve all relevant documents related to a given query. Recall is calculated as the proportion of relevant documents retrieved out of the total number of relevant documents available. For example, if there are twenty relevant documents in the entire dataset, and the system retrieves ten of them, the recall is 0.5 or 50%. A high recall value signifies that the system is comprehensive in fetching relevant information.

However, precision and recall often have an inverse relationship. Improving one may lead to a decrease in the other. To balance this trade-off, the F1 score is used, which is the harmonic mean of precision and recall. The F1 score provides a single measure that considers both metrics, offering a more holistic view of the system's performance. It is particularly useful when the need for a balance between precision and recall is critical.

Another valuable metric is Mean Average Precision (MAP). MAP is particularly useful in scenarios where multiple queries are used to evaluate the system. It calculates the average precision for each query and then takes the mean of these averages. MAP provides a comprehensive measure of the system's performance across a range of queries, offering insights into its consistency and reliability.

To evaluate the ranking quality of the search results, metrics such as Mean Reciprocal Rank (MRR) and Normalized Discounted Cumulative Gain (NDCG) are commonly used. MRR measures the average rank at which the first relevant document is retrieved. For example, if the first relevant document is found at the second position for a query, the reciprocal rank is 0.5. MRR is then calculated as the mean of these reciprocal ranks across multiple queries. A higher MRR indicates that the system is effective at ranking relevant documents higher in the search results.

NDCG, on the other hand, takes into account the position of multiple relevant documents and assigns higher relevance to documents appearing earlier in the search results. It discounts the relevance of documents based on their rank, with higher-ranked documents receiving more weight. NDCG is particularly useful when the order of relevance is important, providing a nuanced view of the system's ranking effectiveness.

User satisfaction is another critical metric that can be measured through various means, such as click-through rates (CTR), dwell time, and user feedback. CTR measures the proportion of users who click on a search result out of the total number of users who viewed the results. High CTR indicates that users find the search results relevant and enticing. Dwell time measures the amount of time users spend on a page after clicking on a search result. Longer dwell times suggest that users find the content useful and engaging. Collecting and analyzing user feedback can also provide valuable insights into the system's performance from the user's perspective.

In addition to these quantitative metrics, qualitative assessments such as user studies and expert evaluations can provide deeper insights into the system's performance. User studies involve observing and analyzing how real users interact with the search system, identifying pain points and areas for improvement. Expert evaluations, on the other hand, involve domain experts assessing the relevance and quality of the search results based on their expertise.

Conclusively, evaluating semantic search systems requires a multifaceted approach that considers various metrics to provide a comprehensive assessment of performance. By leveraging precision, recall, F1 score, MAP, MRR, NDCG, user satisfaction metrics, and qualitative assessments, developers and researchers can gain valuable insights into their systems and make informed decisions to optimize and enhance their search functionalities.

Understanding how users interact with semantic search systems is paramount for both enhancing their experience and improving the system's performance. This section delves into the various techniques and methods used to analyze user interactions, with the ultimate goal of refining and optimizing the search experience.

The first step in analyzing user interaction is to collect comprehensive data on user behavior. This includes tracking search queries, clicks, time spent on pages, and navigation patterns. By gathering this data, developers can build a detailed picture of how users engage with the search system. Tools such as web analytics platforms and custom logging mechanisms are typically employed to capture this information.

Once data collection is in place, the next phase involves analyzing user queries. Query analysis helps identify common search terms, the frequency of specific queries, and patterns in user searches. This analysis can reveal insights into user intent, allowing developers to tailor the search system to better meet user needs. For instance, if a significant number of users are searching for a particular topic, the system can be optimized to provide more relevant results for those queries.

Another critical aspect of user interaction analysis is click-through behavior. By examining which search results users click on, developers can infer the relevance and attractiveness of those results. Click-through data can highlight which results are most useful to users and which ones are being ignored. This information is invaluable for adjusting ranking algorithms and improving the presentation of search results.

In addition to click-through data, dwell time—the amount of time users spend on a particular page after clicking a search result—provides valuable insights into content engagement. Longer dwell times generally indicate that users find the content valuable and relevant to their query. Conversely, short dwell times may suggest that the content did not meet user expectations, prompting a need for further optimization.

User feedback mechanisms, such as ratings and reviews, offer another layer of insight into the user experience. By soliciting direct feedback from users, developers can gain a deeper understanding of their satisfaction and identify specific areas for improvement. Feedback can be collected through various channels, including in-app surveys, feedback forms, and user interviews. Analyzing this qualitative data helps in addressing user pain points and enhancing the overall search experience.

Heatmaps and session recordings are additional tools that provide a visual representation of user interaction. Heatmaps display the areas of a webpage where users click the most, while session recordings capture the entire user journey on a site. These tools can uncover usability issues, such as confusing navigation or ineffective layouts, which may hinder the user experience. By addressing these issues, developers can create a more intuitive and user-friendly search interface.

A/B testing is a powerful technique for optimizing user experience. By presenting different versions of the search interface to different user groups, developers can compare performance metrics and determine which version provides a better experience. A/B tests can be used to evaluate various elements, such as search result layouts, ranking algorithms, or even the wording of search prompts. The insights gained from these tests can drive data-driven decisions for enhancing the search system.

Personalization plays a significant role in improving user interaction with semantic search systems. By leveraging user data, such as past search history and preferences, developers can tailor search results to individual users. Personalization algorithms can rank results based on user-specific factors, increasing the likelihood of presenting relevant content. This individualized approach not only enhances user satisfaction but also encourages continued use of the search system.

Contextual awareness is another crucial aspect of optimizing user interaction. Understanding the context in which a user is searching—such as their location, device, or time of day—can significantly enhance the relevance of search results. For example, a user searching for "restaurants" on a mobile device during lunchtime may be shown nearby dining options. By incorporating contextual factors into the search algorithm, developers can deliver more pertinent results that align with the user's immediate needs.

User interaction analysis also involves studying the overall usability of the search system. Usability testing, where real users perform specific tasks while being observed, can uncover practical issues that may not be evident through data analysis alone. These tests provide direct insights into user challenges and help identify areas where the search system can be streamlined and improved.

To conclude, analyzing user interaction is a multifaceted endeavor that involves collecting and interpreting a wide range of data. By understanding user behavior, preferences, and context, developers can make informed decisions to optimize semantic search systems. The ultimate goal is to create a seamless and satisfying search experience that meets user needs and expectations.

A/B Testing for Search Algorithm Improvements

A/B testing, also known as split testing, is a robust methodology employed to enhance search algorithms by comparing two or more variations of a web page or system functionality. This technique is widely used to determine which version delivers superior performance, thereby enabling data-driven decisions. In the context of semantic search systems, A/B testing serves as an invaluable tool for refining algorithms to provide more accurate and relevant search results.

Before delving into the specifics of A/B testing for search algorithms, it is essential to understand the fundamental principles behind this approach. At its core, A/B testing involves creating two versions of a system component—Version A and Version B—and exposing them to different user groups. By monitoring how each group interacts with their respective versions, developers can collect quantitative data to ascertain which version performs better. This process is iterative, with multiple rounds of testing often conducted to fine-tune the system further.

The first step in implementing A/B testing for search algorithm improvements is to define clear objectives. These objectives could range from enhancing user engagement to increasing click-through rates or improving the overall relevance of search results. Establishing well-defined goals is crucial as it provides a benchmark against which the performance of different algorithmic variations can be measured.

Once the objectives are set, the next phase involves identifying the specific elements of the search algorithm to be tested. These elements could include ranking factors, query interpretation mechanisms, or even the weight assigned to various features inside the algorithm. For instance, one version of the algorithm might prioritize user history more heavily, while another might give greater importance to contextual factors such as location or time of day.

After pinpointing the elements to be tested, the subsequent step is to create the different versions of the search algorithm. This typically involves modifying the existing algorithm to produce the desired variations. It is essential to ensure that these variations are distinct enough to yield meaningful differences in performance metrics. Additionally, careful consideration should be given to maintaining a balance between innovation and stability, as overly radical changes may introduce unforeseen issues.

With the algorithm variations ready, the next critical task is to divide the user base into distinct groups. Randomization is key in this process to ensure that each group is representative of the overall user population. This can be achieved through various techniques, such as random assignment or stratified sampling. The goal is to minimize bias and ensure that the results of the A/B test are generalizable to the entire user base.

Once the user groups are established, the different algorithm versions can be deployed. It is important to monitor the performance of each version in real-time, collecting data on key metrics such as search accuracy, user engagement, and system responsiveness. This data forms the basis for evaluating the effectiveness of each algorithmic variation.

Analyzing the collected data is a critical phase in the A/B testing process. Statistical methods such as t-tests or chi-square tests are commonly used to determine whether the observed differences in performance metrics are statistically significant. This analysis helps in identifying which version of the algorithm meets the predefined objectives more effectively. It is also essential to consider other factors such as user feedback and system stability when making a final decision.

One of the advantages of A/B testing is its iterative nature. Based on the results of the initial test, further refinements can be made to the search algorithm, and additional rounds of testing can be conducted. This iterative process allows for continuous improvement, ensuring that the search system evolves to meet changing user needs and preferences.

In addition to improving the search algorithm, A/B testing can also provide valuable insights into user behavior. By examining how different user groups interact with various algorithmic versions, developers can gain a deeper understanding of user preferences and search patterns. This information can be leveraged to make more informed decisions about future algorithmic changes and enhancements.

However, A/B testing is not without its challenges. One of the primary concerns is the potential for introducing bias into the test results. This can occur if the user groups are not truly representative of the overall user base or if external factors influence the test outcomes. To mitigate this risk, it is essential to employ rigorous randomization techniques and to conduct the tests over a sufficiently long period to account for variability in user behavior.

Another challenge is the need for significant computational resources. Running multiple versions of a search algorithm simultaneously can be resource-intensive, requiring robust infrastructure to handle the increased load. It is important to ensure that the testing environment is stable and that any performance issues are promptly addressed.

Despite these challenges, the benefits of A/B testing for search algorithm improvements far outweigh the drawbacks. By providing a systematic and data-driven approach to refining search algorithms, A/B testing helps developers create more effective and user-centric search systems. The iterative nature of the process ensures that the search system continuously evolves, adapting to changing user needs and technological advancements.

In summary, A/B testing is a powerful technique for optimizing search algorithms in semantic search systems. By defining clear objectives, creating distinct algorithm variations, and rigorously analyzing performance data, developers can make informed decisions that enhance the overall search experience. While challenges such as potential bias and resource requirements must be addressed, the insights gained from A/B testing are invaluable in creating a more accurate and relevant search system.

In semantic search systems, error analysis and debugging are pivotal processes that ensure the integrity and efficacy of the search functionalities. These processes are indispensable for identifying, diagnosing, and rectifying issues that may arise inside the system. This section delves into the methodologies and strategies for conducting thorough error analysis and effective debugging, providing a roadmap for developers to enhance their semantic search systems.

The initial step in error analysis is the identification of anomalies and inconsistencies inside the search results. Anomalies can manifest in various forms, such as irrelevant results, missing relevant documents, or unexpected system behavior. To systematically identify these issues, developers often employ a combination of automated testing and manual review. Automated testing involves running predefined test cases that cover a broad spectrum of queries and scenarios. These test cases are designed to trigger potential edge cases and identify deviations from expected outcomes. Manual review, on the other hand, entails a more nuanced examination of search results to catch subtleties that automated tests might miss.

Once anomalies are identified, the next phase involves diagnosing the root causes of these issues. This diagnostic process requires a deep understanding of the underlying algorithms and data structures that power the semantic search system. One effective approach is to conduct a component-wise analysis, where each segment of the search pipeline is scrutinized independently. This includes examining the data preprocessing steps, the feature extraction mechanisms, and the ranking algorithms. By isolating each component, developers can pinpoint the exact stage where the error originates, thereby narrowing down the scope of the investigation.

Log analysis is another critical tool in the diagnostic arsenal. Detailed logs provide a chronological record of system activities, capturing vital information about the execution flow and intermediate states. By analyzing these logs, developers can trace the sequence of operations leading up to the anomaly, uncovering patterns and correlations that might elucidate the root cause. Log analysis tools, equipped with advanced filtering and search capabilities, can significantly expedite this process, enabling developers to sift through vast volumes of data efficiently.

Debugging, the process of rectifying identified issues, often begins with the formulation of hypotheses about the potential causes of the anomaly. These hypotheses are then tested iteratively, with each iteration involving a modification to the system and a subsequent evaluation of its impact. This iterative process, known as the scientific method of debugging, allows developers to systematically converge towards the root cause and implement a targeted fix. It is essential to document each hypothesis and its corresponding test results meticulously, as this documentation serves as a valuable reference for future debugging efforts.

One of the common challenges in debugging semantic search systems is the inherent complexity of the algorithms involved. These algorithms often leverage sophisticated techniques such as deep learning and natural language processing, which can introduce layers of abstraction and non-linearity. To mitigate this complexity, developers can employ visualization techniques that provide intuitive representations of the algorithm's internal states. For instance, visualizing the attention weights in a neural network can reveal which parts of the input data are influencing the model's decisions, thereby shedding light on potential sources of error.

In addition to visualizations, interactive debugging tools can offer real-time insights into the system's behavior. These tools allow developers to set breakpoints, inspect variable states, and step through the execution flow interactively. By providing a granular level of control over the debugging process, interactive tools facilitate a more detailed examination of the system's internals, enabling developers to uncover subtle issues that might otherwise go unnoticed.

Another effective debugging technique is the use of synthetic data. Synthetic data, generated artificially to mimic real-world scenarios, allows developers to create controlled environments for testing specific aspects of the system. By manipulating the characteristics of the synthetic data, developers can isolate and stress-test individual components, revealing how they respond under various conditions. This approach is particularly useful for identifying edge cases and rare scenarios that might not be adequately represented in the real-world data.

Collaboration and peer review are also invaluable in the debugging process. Engaging multiple perspectives can uncover blind spots and introduce fresh insights that might otherwise be overlooked. Code reviews, where peers examine the codebase and provide feedback, can highlight potential issues and suggest alternative solutions. Pair programming, where two developers work together on the same code, fosters a collaborative environment that encourages knowledge sharing and collective problem-solving.

In sum, error analysis and debugging are critical processes for maintaining the robustness and reliability of semantic search systems. By systematically identifying anomalies, diagnosing root causes, and employing a combination of automated tools, visualizations, interactive debugging techniques, and collaborative practices, developers can effectively address issues and optimize their systems. These methodologies not only enhance the performance of the search functionalities but also contribute to a deeper understanding of the underlying algorithms, paving the way for continuous improvement and innovation in semantic search technology.

In semantic search systems, optimizing query processing and response times is essential for delivering a seamless and efficient user experience. The speed and accuracy with which a search system can interpret and respond to user queries significantly impact user satisfaction and engagement. This section explores various strategies and techniques to enhance the performance of query processing and minimize response times, ensuring that users receive prompt and relevant results.

The first step in optimizing query processing involves streamlining the query interpretation mechanism. This process typically includes parsing the user's input, identifying key terms, and understanding the context of the query. To achieve this, developers can employ advanced natural language processing (NLP) techniques such as tokenization, part-of-speech tagging, and named entity recognition. By accurately dissecting the query into its constituent parts, the system can more efficiently map the user's intent to relevant search results. Additionally, leveraging pre-trained language models can expedite this process, as they provide a robust foundation for understanding diverse and complex queries.

Another crucial aspect of query processing optimization is the implementation of efficient data indexing techniques. Indexing involves creating a structured representation of the data, allowing for rapid retrieval of information. Traditional inverted index structures, which map terms to their corresponding documents, can be enhanced with more sophisticated data structures like B-trees or Tries. These structures facilitate faster lookups and reduce the computational overhead associated with searching large datasets. Moreover, incorporating techniques such as term frequency-inverse document frequency (TF-IDF) can help prioritize the most relevant documents, further improving retrieval efficiency.

Caching mechanisms play a pivotal role in reducing response times by storing frequently accessed data in memory. Query caching involves saving the results of commonly executed queries, enabling the system to quickly return results without reprocessing the query from scratch. This approach is particularly effective for queries with high repetition rates, as it significantly reduces the computational load on the system. Additionally, implementing a multi-tiered caching strategy, where data is cached at various levels (e.g., in-memory, disk-based), can further enhance performance by balancing speed and storage efficiency.

Parallel processing and distributed computing frameworks are indispensable tools for optimizing query processing in large-scale semantic search systems. By distributing the workload across multiple processors or nodes, these frameworks enable concurrent execution of query-related tasks, thereby reducing overall response times. Technologies such as Apache Hadoop and Apache Spark provide robust platforms for implementing distributed processing, allowing the system to handle massive datasets and complex queries with ease. Furthermore, leveraging load balancing techniques ensures an even distribution of tasks, preventing any single node from becoming a bottleneck.

Another strategy for optimizing query processing is the use of query rewriting techniques. Query rewriting involves transforming the original user query into a more efficient or semantically equivalent form that is easier to process. This can include techniques such as query expansion, where additional relevant terms are added to the query, or query reduction, where unnecessary terms are removed. By refining the query in this manner, the system can improve the precision and recall of search results while reducing the computational effort required to process the query.

Optimizing the underlying hardware and infrastructure is also critical for achieving low response times. Investing in high-performance servers, solid-state drives (SSDs), and ample memory resources can significantly enhance the system's ability to process queries swiftly. Additionally, employing techniques such as data partitioning and replication can improve data access speed and fault tolerance. By strategically distributing data across multiple storage devices and locations, the system can ensure rapid retrieval and resilience against hardware failures.

Monitoring and analyzing system performance metrics is essential for identifying bottlenecks and areas for improvement in query processing. Tools such as performance profilers and monitoring dashboards provide real-time insights into various aspects of the system, including CPU usage, memory consumption, and query execution times. By continuously tracking these metrics, developers can pinpoint specific components or processes that are causing delays and take corrective actions. Regular performance audits and stress testing can further help in maintaining optimal system performance under varying loads and usage patterns.

Implementing machine learning models for query optimization is an emerging trend that holds significant promise. Machine learning algorithms can analyze historical query data to identify patterns and predict the most efficient processing strategies for future queries. For instance, reinforcement learning models can dynamically adjust query execution plans based on real-time feedback, continuously optimizing the system's performance. Additionally, machine learning techniques can be used to develop predictive caching strategies, where the system anticipates and preloads data for queries that are likely to be executed, further reducing response times.

Finally, user experience considerations should not be overlooked when optimizing query processing and response times. Providing users with immediate feedback, such as displaying query suggestions or partial results while the full query is being processed, can enhance the perceived responsiveness of the system. Additionally, implementing asynchronous processing techniques, where long-running queries are executed in the background and users are notified upon completion, can improve overall user satisfaction. By balancing technical optimizations with user-centric design, developers can create a search system that is both efficient and engaging.

To conclude, optimizing query processing and response times in semantic search systems is a multifaceted endeavor that requires a combination of advanced algorithms, efficient data structures, robust infrastructure, and continuous performance monitoring. By employing a holistic approach that integrates these elements, developers can create search systems that deliver fast, accurate, and relevant results, ultimately enhancing the user experience and driving engagement. The strategies and techniques discussed in this section provide a comprehensive framework for achieving these optimization goals, ensuring that semantic search systems remain responsive and effective in meeting user needs.

In semantic search systems, continuous improvement is paramount for maintaining and enhancing the relevance and accuracy of search results. One of the most effective methodologies for achieving this is the implementation of feedback loops. Feedback loops serve as a dynamic mechanism that allows systems to learn from user interactions and evolve over time. This section explores the intricacies of utilizing feedback loops to foster ongoing enhancements in semantic search systems, ensuring they remain aligned with user expectations and technological advancements.

The concept of feedback loops is rooted in the idea of using output from a system to inform and refine its future performance. In the context of semantic search, this involves collecting data on how users interact with search results and using this information to make iterative adjustments to the search algorithms. The process begins with the collection of user feedback, which can be explicit or implicit. Explicit feedback is directly provided by users, often in the form of ratings, comments, or selections indicating the relevance of search results. Implicit feedback, on the other hand, is inferred from user behaviors such as click-through rates, dwell time on pages, and search abandonment rates.

Once feedback data is collected, the next step is to analyze it to identify patterns and insights. This analysis can reveal valuable information about user preferences, common search queries, and areas where the search system may be underperforming. Advanced analytical techniques, including machine learning algorithms and statistical analysis, can be employed to detect trends and correlations in the feedback data. These insights form the foundation for making informed adjustments to the search algorithms.

One of the key advantages of feedback loops is their ability to facilitate personalized search experiences. By continuously analyzing user feedback, semantic search systems can tailor search results to individual users based on their past interactions and preferences. For example, if a user frequently clicks on certain types of documents or spends more time on specific topics, the system can prioritize similar content in future search results. This personalization enhances user satisfaction by delivering more relevant and meaningful search experiences.

Another critical aspect of utilizing feedback loops is the implementation of a robust feedback collection mechanism. This involves designing user interfaces and interactions that encourage users to provide feedback without disrupting their search experience. For explicit feedback, this could include features such as thumbs-up/thumbs-down buttons, star ratings, or feedback forms. For implicit feedback, it is essential to track user interactions seamlessly, ensuring that the data collected is accurate and representative of genuine user behavior. Privacy and ethical considerations must also be addressed, ensuring that users are aware of how their data is being used and that their privacy is protected.

Feedback loops also play a crucial role in identifying and mitigating biases in semantic search systems. Biases can arise from various sources, including biased training data, algorithmic biases, and user biases. By continuously monitoring feedback and analyzing discrepancies in search results, developers can detect and address biases that may impact the fairness and inclusivity of the search system. For instance, if certain user groups consistently receive less relevant results, this could indicate a bias that needs to be corrected. Implementing feedback loops allows for proactive detection and rectification of such issues, promoting a more equitable search experience for all users.

The iterative nature of feedback loops aligns well with the principles of agile development and continuous integration. In an agile framework, feedback loops can be integrated into the development cycle, enabling regular updates and refinements to the search algorithms based on real-time user feedback. This approach ensures that the search system remains adaptable and responsive to changing user needs and technological advancements. Regular sprints and releases allow for incremental improvements, fostering a culture of continuous innovation and enhancement.

Moreover, feedback loops can be leveraged to conduct experiments and validate hypotheses about search algorithm improvements. By implementing A/B testing or multivariate testing, developers can compare different versions of search algorithms and evaluate their performance based on user feedback. These experiments provide empirical evidence on the effectiveness of proposed changes, enabling data-driven decision-making and reducing the risk of unintended consequences. Feedback loops thus serve as a valuable tool for experimentation and validation, driving informed and evidence-based improvements.

In addition to algorithmic adjustments, feedback loops can also inform content curation and indexing strategies. By analyzing user feedback, developers can identify gaps in the search index and prioritize the inclusion of high-demand content. For example, if users frequently search for specific topics or documents that are not well-represented in the index, this indicates a need to expand the index to include relevant content. Feedback loops ensure that the search system remains comprehensive and up-to-date, aligning with user interests and information needs.

Implementing effective feedback loops requires a collaborative effort involving cross-functional teams, including data scientists, developers, user experience designers, and domain experts. Collaboration fosters a holistic understanding of user feedback, ensuring that insights are interpreted accurately and translated into actionable improvements. Regular meetings and knowledge-sharing sessions can facilitate communication and coordination, promoting a unified approach to continuous improvement.

Lastly, it is essential to establish clear metrics and key performance indicators (KPIs) to measure the impact of feedback loops on the search system's performance. Metrics such as user satisfaction scores, relevance ratings, search success rates, and time-to-result can provide quantitative insights into the effectiveness of feedback-driven improvements. Continuous monitoring and evaluation of these metrics allow for ongoing assessment and optimization, ensuring that the feedback loops deliver tangible benefits.

In conclusion, utilizing feedback loops for continuous improvement is a powerful strategy for enhancing semantic search systems. By systematically collecting, analyzing, and acting on user feedback, developers can create search experiences that are increasingly relevant, personalized, and user-centric. Feedback loops enable iterative refinements, promote personalization, mitigate biases, and support agile development practices. Through collaboration and the use of advanced analytical techniques, feedback loops drive ongoing innovation and ensure that semantic search systems remain responsive to user needs and technological advancements.

In the evolving landscape of information retrieval, the ability to scale search systems effectively is paramount. As data volumes grow exponentially, ensuring that semantic search systems can handle increased loads without compromising performance becomes a critical challenge. This section delves into the key considerations and strategies for achieving scalability in large-scale search systems, offering a comprehensive guide for developers aiming to create robust and efficient search solutions.

One of the foundational elements of scalable search systems is the architecture. A well-designed architecture can accommodate growth in both data and user queries. Distributed architectures, where the workload is spread across multiple servers or nodes, are particularly effective. These architectures leverage the power of parallel processing, enabling the system to manage large datasets and numerous queries simultaneously. By distributing tasks, the system can avoid bottlenecks and maintain high performance even under heavy loads.

An essential aspect of this distributed approach is data partitioning. Partitioning involves dividing the dataset into smaller, more manageable chunks, often referred to as shards. Each shard can be stored and processed independently, allowing for concurrent access and retrieval. Effective partitioning strategies consider factors such as data distribution, access patterns, and query complexity. Horizontal partitioning, where data is divided based on specific criteria such as date ranges or categories, can enhance retrieval efficiency and ensure balanced load distribution across nodes.

In addition to partitioning, replication plays a crucial role in scalability. Replication involves creating multiple copies of data across different nodes. This not only enhances data availability and fault tolerance but also improves read performance. When multiple replicas are available, read requests can be distributed among them, reducing the load on individual nodes and speeding up query response times. However, managing data consistency across replicas requires careful coordination, often implemented through consensus algorithms or replication protocols.

Another significant consideration for scalability is the indexing mechanism. Efficient indexing enables rapid search and retrieval, even as the dataset grows. Traditional indexing techniques, such as inverted indexes, remain relevant, but they must be optimized for large-scale environments. Advanced indexing structures, like hierarchical or multi-level indexes, can further enhance performance by organizing data in a way that minimizes search time. Additionally, leveraging modern data structures such as Bloom filters or skip lists can reduce the computational overhead associated with indexing and querying large datasets.

Caching mechanisms are indispensable for improving scalability. By storing frequently accessed data in memory, caches can significantly reduce the time required to process repetitive queries. Multi-tiered caching strategies, where data is cached at different levels (e.g., in-memory, disk-based), provide a balance between speed and storage efficiency. Implementing intelligent caching policies that consider query frequency, data freshness, and resource availability can optimize cache utilization and enhance overall system performance.

Load balancing is another critical factor in scalable search systems. Effective load balancing ensures that the workload is evenly distributed across all nodes, preventing any single node from becoming a performance bottleneck. Dynamic load balancing techniques, which adjust the distribution of tasks in real-time based on current load and resource utilization, are particularly effective. These techniques can adapt to changing conditions, such as fluctuating query volumes or varying data access patterns, ensuring consistent performance under diverse scenarios.

Furthermore, the choice of hardware and infrastructure has a profound impact on scalability. Investing in high-performance servers, solid-state drives (SSDs), and ample memory resources can significantly enhance the system's ability to handle large-scale operations. Cloud-based solutions offer scalable infrastructure that can be adjusted dynamically based on demand. By leveraging cloud services, developers can scale resources up or down as needed, ensuring optimal performance without over-provisioning.

Monitoring and performance analysis are essential for maintaining scalability. Continuous monitoring of system metrics, such as query response times, CPU and memory usage, and network latency, provides valuable insights into the system's performance. Performance analysis tools can help identify bottlenecks, resource constraints, and other issues that may impact scalability. Regular performance audits and stress testing can ensure that the system remains capable of handling increased loads and can guide future scalability enhancements.

Implementing scalability in large-scale search systems also involves optimizing algorithms and query processing techniques. Efficient algorithms that minimize computational complexity and resource consumption are vital. Techniques such as query rewriting, where complex queries are transformed into simpler, more efficient forms, can enhance processing

148

speed and reduce resource usage. Additionally, employing machine learning models to predict and optimize query execution plans can further improve scalability by adapting to changing data and query patterns.

Finally, scalability considerations must also address the user experience. As the system scales, maintaining a seamless and responsive user experience is crucial. Providing users with real-time feedback, such as displaying query suggestions or partial results while the full query is being processed, can enhance perceived responsiveness. Asynchronous processing techniques, where long-running queries are executed in the background and users are notified upon completion, can improve user satisfaction and engagement.

In summary, achieving scalability in large-scale search systems is a multifaceted endeavor that requires a holistic approach. By focusing on architectural design, data partitioning and replication, efficient indexing, caching mechanisms, load balancing, infrastructure optimization, continuous monitoring, algorithmic efficiency, and user experience, developers can create search systems that are both robust and scalable. These strategies ensure that the system can handle increasing data volumes and query loads without compromising performance, ultimately delivering a seamless and efficient search experience for users.

Advanced Topics: Contextual Understanding And Query Expansion

Understanding Contextual Relevance in Semantic Search

Contextual relevance is a cornerstone of effective semantic search systems. It involves understanding the context inside which a query is made to deliver results that are not just syntactically correct but semantically meaningful. This section delves into the intricacies of contextual relevance, exploring how semantic search engines interpret and leverage context to improve search outcomes.

To begin with, contextual relevance requires a comprehensive grasp of user intent. Unlike traditional keyword-based search systems, which rely heavily on exact term matches, semantic search engines analyze the broader context in which a query exists. For instance, consider the query "apple." In a keyword-based system, the term "apple" might return results about the fruit, the technology company, or even a popular dessert recipe. However, a semantic search engine would evaluate the surrounding context—such as the user's previous queries, location, and browsing history—to determine whether the user is more likely interested in the fruit, the corporation, or something entirely different.

One of the primary methods for achieving contextual relevance is through natural language processing (NLP). NLP techniques enable search engines to parse and understand the nuances of human language. By analyzing syntax, semantics, and even sentiment, NLP helps in deciphering the true intent behind a query. For example, the query "best apple in New York" would be interpreted differently based on whether the user is searching for the best apple fruit or the best Apple store in New York City. Through NLP, the search engine can distinguish between these contexts and provide results that align more closely with what the user is seeking.

Another critical aspect of contextual relevance is the use of knowledge graphs. Knowledge graphs are structured representations of information that link entities and their relationships. These graphs help semantic search engines understand the connections between different pieces of information, enabling more accurate and contextually relevant search results. For instance, if a user queries "Shakespeare birthplace," a knowledge graph can help the search engine connect the dots between William Shakespeare, his birthplace in Stratford-upon-Avon, and relevant historical data. This interconnected understanding allows for a richer and more pertinent set of search outcomes.

Contextual relevance also benefits from the incorporation of machine learning algorithms. These algorithms can analyze vast amounts of data to identify patterns and trends that might not be immediately apparent. By learning from user interactions and feedback, machine learning models can continually refine their understanding of context, improving the accuracy of search results over time. For example, if a user frequently searches for information related to technology, the search engine can learn to prioritize tech-related results for ambiguous queries, thereby enhancing the overall search experience.

Furthermore, contextual relevance is significantly enhanced by personalized search experiences. Personalization involves tailoring search results based on individual user preferences, behavior, and history. By leveraging data such as past searches, clicks, and even social media activity, semantic search engines can deliver results that are more aligned with each user's unique context. For instance, a user who often searches for vegan recipes might receive more relevant results for a query like "best burger recipe" compared to someone with a different set of interests.

In addition to personalization, the role of real-time data cannot be overstated in achieving contextual relevance. Real-time data allows semantic search engines to adapt to the current context quickly. For instance, if a user searches for "current weather," the search engine can provide up-to-date weather information based on the user's location at that precise moment. This dynamic adaptation ensures that the search results remain relevant and timely, enhancing the overall user experience.

The challenges of contextual relevance are not insignificant. One of the primary hurdles is the ambiguity inherent in human language. Words and phrases can have multiple meanings, and without proper context, it can be challenging to discern the correct interpretation. Additionally, privacy concerns arise when dealing with personalized data. Balancing the need for contextual relevance with the protection of user privacy is a delicate task that requires careful consideration and robust safeguards.

Despite these challenges, the benefits of achieving contextual relevance in semantic search are substantial. Users are more likely to find the information they need quickly and efficiently, leading to higher satisfaction and engagement. For businesses, this translates to better customer experiences and potentially higher conversion rates.

To conclude, understanding and implementing contextual relevance is essential for the success of semantic search systems. By leveraging techniques such as natural language processing, knowledge graphs, machine learning, and personalization, search engines can deliver results that are not only accurate but also deeply meaningful to the user. As technology continues to evolve, the ability to understand and respond to context will become increasingly critical, shaping the future of search in profound ways.

Enhancing the understanding of user queries is a vital component in refining the effectiveness of semantic search systems. This section explores various techniques that contribute to a more nuanced comprehension of user queries, facilitating more accurate and relevant search results. By leveraging these techniques, search engines can better interpret the underlying intent and context of queries, thereby providing users with a more satisfying search experience.

One of the fundamental techniques for enhancing query understanding is the use of linguistic analysis. Linguistic analysis involves examining the structure and meaning of language components inside a query. This includes parsing the syntax, identifying parts of speech, and recognizing named entities. For example, a query like "top universities in Europe" can be broken down into its linguistic components to understand that "top" is a superlative adjective, "universities" is a noun, and "Europe" is a named entity referring to a geographic region. By dissecting the query in this manner, search engines can better grasp the user's intent and provide more targeted results.

Another essential technique is the application of semantic parsing. Semantic parsing goes beyond mere syntactic analysis by interpreting the meaning of the query in a more profound sense. It involves translating the natural language input into a machine-readable format, such as a logical form or a set of structured data. For instance, the query "find books by J.K. Rowling" can be semantically parsed to identify "books" as the subject and "J.K. Rowling" as the author. This structured representation allows the search engine to precisely match the query with relevant data in its index, leading to more accurate search outcomes.

Contextual analysis is another powerful technique that enhances query understanding. This involves considering the broader context in which the query is made, including the user's previous interactions, location, and temporal factors. For example, if a user frequently searches for information related to travel, a query like "best places to visit" can be interpreted in the context of travel interests, leading to more relevant suggestions. Additionally, contextual analysis can account for seasonal variations, such as interpreting "holiday destinations" differently in summer versus winter. By incorporating contextual factors, search engines can tailor their responses to better align with the user's current needs and preferences.

Query expansion is a technique that aims to improve query understanding by broadening the scope of the original query. This can be achieved through various methods, such as synonym expansion, where synonyms of the query terms are added to the search. For instance, a query for "car repair" can be expanded to include "automobile repair" and "vehicle maintenance," thereby increasing the chances of retrieving relevant results. Another method is using related terms and concepts to enhance the query. For example, a query about "heart disease" could be expanded to include related terms like "cardiovascular disease" and "coronary artery disease." Query expansion helps in overcoming the limitations of short or ambiguous queries, providing a richer set of search results.

Machine learning algorithms play a crucial role in enhancing query understanding. These algorithms can analyze large datasets to identify patterns and trends that inform the interpretation of queries. For example, by training on a vast corpus of search queries and user interactions, machine learning models can learn to recognize common query patterns and their associated intents. This enables the search engine to predict the most likely intent behind a new query and retrieve relevant results accordingly. Additionally, machine learning models can continuously improve over time by incorporating feedback and learning from user behavior, leading to increasingly accurate query understanding.

Another advanced technique is the use of query rewriting. Query rewriting involves transforming the original query into a different form that is more likely to yield relevant results. This can include rephrasing the query, correcting spelling errors, and resolving ambiguities. For instance, a query like "how to fix a leaky faucet" can be rewritten as "leaky faucet repair guide" to better match the content available in the search index. Query rewriting helps bridge the gap between the user's natural language input and the structured data in the search engine's database, enhancing the overall search experience.

Knowledge graphs are also instrumental in enhancing query understanding. Knowledge graphs are structured representations of information that link entities and their relationships. By leveraging knowledge graphs, search engines can gain a deeper understanding of the connections between different concepts and entities. For example, a query about "Albert Einstein" can be enriched with information about his contributions to physics, his famous theories, and his biographical details. This interconnected understanding allows the search engine to provide more comprehensive and contextually rich search results.

Incorporating user feedback is another valuable technique for enhancing query understanding. By analyzing user interactions and feedback, search engines can gain insights into how well their interpretations of queries align with user expectations. For example, if users frequently refine their queries or click on specific types of results, the search engine can learn from these behaviors and adjust its query understanding algorithms accordingly. User feedback serves as a continuous loop of improvement, ensuring that the search engine evolves to better meet user needs over time.

In sum, enhancing query understanding is a multifaceted endeavor that involves a range of techniques, from linguistic analysis and semantic parsing to contextual analysis and query expansion. By leveraging machine learning, query rewriting, knowledge graphs, and user feedback, search engines can achieve a deeper and more accurate comprehension of user queries. These advancements not only improve the relevance and quality of search results but also contribute to a more intuitive and satisfying search experience for users. As technology continues to advance, the techniques for enhancing query understanding will undoubtedly evolve, further pushing the boundaries of what semantic search systems can achieve.

In semantic search, the ability to harness contextual signals significantly enhances the relevance and accuracy of search results. Contextual signals refer to the various pieces of information and cues that provide insight into the user's intent and the environment in which a query is made. By effectively leveraging these signals, search engines can deliver results that are not only pertinent but also precisely aligned with the user's needs at the moment.

To begin with, one of the most fundamental sources of context is the user's search history. By analyzing past queries, search engines can discern patterns and preferences that inform the interpretation of new queries. For instance, if a user frequently searches for topics related to health and wellness, a query about "benefits of green tea" can be understood inside that specific context, leading to results that emphasize health benefits rather than culinary uses. This historical data provides a foundation upon which more nuanced interpretations can be built, allowing for a tailored search experience.

Another critical aspect of contextual signals is the temporal context. The time at which a query is made can significantly influence its meaning and relevance. For example, a search for "holiday recipes" in December is likely to pertain to festive dishes for Christmas or Hanukkah, whereas the same query in November might be more aligned with Thanksgiving. By incorporating temporal information, search engines can adjust their algorithms to prioritize results that are seasonally appropriate, thereby enhancing the user's experience.

Geographic location is another powerful contextual signal that can drastically alter the relevance of search results. A query for "best coffee shops" will yield different results depending on whether the user is in Seattle, Paris, or Tokyo. By leveraging geolocation data, search engines can provide localized results that are directly relevant to the user's immediate surroundings. This localization not only improves the utility of the search results but also fosters a more personalized and engaging search experience.

Social context, derived from social media activity and connections, is another valuable source of contextual signals. By analyzing the user's interactions on platforms such as Facebook, Twitter, and LinkedIn, search engines can gain insights into their interests, affiliations, and social circles. For instance, if a user is part of multiple online communities focused on technology, a query about "latest gadgets" can be interpreted with an emphasis on cutting-edge innovations and industry trends. This social context allows for a more refined understanding of the user's intent, leading to search results that are more closely aligned with their interests and preferences.

Device context also plays a significant role in interpreting queries. The type of device being used—whether it's a smartphone, tablet, or desktop computer—can influence the kind of results that are most relevant. For example, a query for "directions to the nearest gas station" made on a smartphone is likely seeking immediate, location-based directions, while the same query on a desktop might be part of broader trip planning. By considering the device context, search engines can tailor their responses to better suit the user's current needs and circumstances.

Another important contextual signal is the user's behavioral patterns. This includes data on how users interact with search results, such as click-through rates, dwell time, and bounce

159

rates. By analyzing these behaviors, search engines can infer which types of results are most useful and engaging for the user. For instance, if a user consistently clicks on video content rather than text articles, a query for "how to tie a tie" might prioritize video tutorials over written instructions. These behavioral insights enable search engines to continuously refine their algorithms, ensuring that the results remain relevant and engaging over time.

In addition to these individual contextual signals, the integration of multiple signals can lead to even more sophisticated interpretations of user queries. For example, a query for "good restaurants" made on a Friday evening from a smartphone in downtown New York, by a user who frequently checks in at high-end dining establishments on social media, can be understood with a high degree of specificity. The search engine can infer that the user is likely looking for upscale dining options available in real-time, and prioritize results accordingly. This multi-faceted approach to contextual understanding allows for a level of precision that would be unattainable using isolated signals.

The use of contextual signals is not without its challenges. One of the primary concerns is the balance between personalization and privacy. Leveraging detailed contextual data requires accessing and processing potentially sensitive information, raising concerns about data security and user consent. Ensuring that users are aware of how their data is being used and providing them with control over their privacy settings is essential in maintaining trust and compliance with regulations.

Another challenge lies in the inherent complexity and variability of human language. Contextual signals can help disambiguate queries, but they are not foolproof. Ambiguities and nuances in language can still lead to misinterpretations, necessitating ongoing advancements in natural language processing and machine learning techniques. Moreover, the dynamic nature of context means that search engines must be capable of adapting to changing circumstances in real-time, which requires robust and responsive algorithms.

Despite these challenges, the benefits of leveraging contextual signals for improved search results are substantial. By incorporating historical, temporal, geographic, social, device, and behavioral contexts, search engines can deliver results that are more accurate, relevant, and personalized. This enhanced relevance not only improves user satisfaction but also increases engagement and retention, providing significant advantages for both users and service providers.

In conclusion, the effective use of contextual signals is a cornerstone of advanced semantic search systems. By understanding and integrating various forms of context, search engines can move beyond simple keyword matching to provide results that truly resonate with the user's intent and circumstances. As technology continues to evolve, the ability to leverage contextual signals will become increasingly sophisticated, paving the way for ever more intuitive and effective search experiences.

Query expansion stands as a crucial technique in the realm of semantic search, aiming to enhance the retrieval of relevant information by broadening the scope of user queries. This section delves into advanced methods of query expansion, exploring techniques that go beyond basic synonym addition to include sophisticated algorithms and contextual considerations. These methods collectively contribute to more accurate and comprehensive search results, ultimately improving user satisfaction.

One of the advanced methods in query expansion involves leveraging word embeddings. Word embeddings are dense vector representations of words that capture their semantic meanings based on their context in large text corpora. Techniques such as Word2Vec, GloVe, and FastText have revolutionized the way machines understand human language. By mapping words to a continuous vector space, these embeddings enable the identification of words that are semantically similar, even if they do not share the same lexical root. For example, the words "car," "automobile," and "vehicle" might be close to each other in the vector space, allowing the search engine to expand a query containing "car" to include "automobile" and "vehicle," thereby retrieving a broader set of relevant documents.

Another sophisticated approach to query expansion is the use of topic modeling. Topic modeling algorithms, such as Latent Dirichlet Allocation (LDA) and Non-negative Matrix Factorization (NMF), uncover hidden themes inside a corpus of documents. By identifying the underlying topics associated with a query, these models can suggest additional terms that are contextually relevant. For instance, a query about "climate change" might be expanded to include terms like "global warming," "carbon emissions," and "renewable energy," based on the topics prevalent in the relevant documents. This thematic expansion ensures that the search engine captures a wider array of pertinent information.

Graph-based query expansion is another advanced method that leverages the power of network structures. In this approach, entities and their relationships are represented as nodes and edges in a graph. Techniques like Personalized PageRank and HITS (Hyperlink-Induced Topic Search) can be used to identify important and contextually relevant nodes connected to the original query terms. For example, in a query about "quantum computing," a graph-based approach might identify related concepts such as "qubits," "superposition," and "entanglement," expanding the query to encompass these terms. This method is particularly effective in domains with rich interconnections between concepts, such as scientific research and technical fields.

Contextual query expansion takes into account the broader context in which a query is made. This method involves analyzing user behavior, preferences, and situational factors to tailor the expansion process. Techniques such as machine learning models trained on user interaction data can predict additional terms that align with the user's intent and context. For instance, if a user frequently searches for topics related to digital marketing, a query about "SEO strategies" might be expanded to include terms like "content marketing," "link building," and "keyword research." By incorporating contextual data, this approach ensures that the expanded query remains relevant to the user's specific interests and needs.

Temporal query expansion is another advanced technique that considers the time dimension of a query. The relevance of certain terms can vary over time, and temporal query expansion aims to capture these dynamics. For example, a query about "Olympics" in

2021 would likely benefit from expansion to include terms like "Tokyo 2020," "Olympic Games," and "medal tally." Temporal models can analyze historical data and trends to identify terms that are temporally aligned with the query, ensuring that the search results are up-to-date and contextually appropriate.

Probabilistic models for query expansion represent another sophisticated approach. Techniques such as probabilistic latent semantic analysis (PLSA) and Bayesian networks use statistical methods to model the relationships between terms and documents. By estimating the probabilities of terms co-occurring with the original query terms, these models can suggest additional terms that are likely to be relevant. For instance, a query about "machine learning" might be expanded to include terms like "neural networks," "supervised learning," and "unsupervised learning," based on their probabilistic associations with the original query. This method leverages the power of statistics to enhance the query expansion process.

Interactive query expansion involves user participation in the expansion process. In this approach, the search engine presents the user with a list of suggested terms related to their query, allowing them to select the terms that best match their intent. This method can be particularly effective in cases where the user's intent is ambiguous or multifaceted. For example, a query about "baking recipes" might prompt the user to choose between terms like "cakes," "cookies," and "bread," refining the search to better align with their specific interest. By incorporating user feedback, interactive query expansion ensures that the expanded query is closely aligned with the user's needs.

Domain-specific query expansion tailors the expansion process to the unique characteristics of a particular field or industry. This method involves creating specialized lexicons, ontologies, and knowledge bases that capture the terminology and relationships specific to the domain. For example, in the medical field, a query about "diabetes treatment" might be expanded to include terms like "insulin therapy," "blood sugar management," and "diabetic diet," based on a domain-specific knowledge base. This approach ensures that the expanded query is highly relevant to the specific domain, improving the precision of the search results.

Another advanced method is the use of query logs for expansion. Query logs contain historical data on user queries and their corresponding search results. By analyzing these logs, search engines can identify common query reformulations and expansions used by other users. For instance, if many users who initially searched for "smartphone" later refined their query to include terms like "iPhone" or "Android," the search engine can use this information to automatically expand similar queries in the future. Query log analysis leverages collective user behavior to inform the expansion process, enhancing the relevance of the search results.

Finally, hybrid approaches to query expansion combine multiple methods to achieve the best results. By integrating techniques such as word embeddings, topic modeling, graph-based methods, and user feedback, hybrid approaches can leverage the strengths of each method while mitigating their individual limitations. For example, a hybrid approach might use word embeddings to identify semantically similar terms, topic modeling to uncover relevant themes, and user feedback to refine the final set of expanded terms. This comprehensive approach ensures that the query expansion process is robust, flexible, and highly effective.

To conclude, advanced query expansion methods play a pivotal role in enhancing the effectiveness of semantic search systems. By leveraging techniques such as word embeddings, topic modeling, graph-based methods, contextual analysis, temporal models, probabilistic models, interactive expansion, domain-specific knowledge, query logs, and hybrid approaches, search engines can achieve a deeper and more nuanced understanding of user queries. These methods collectively contribute to more accurate, relevant, and comprehensive search results, ultimately improving the user experience and satisfaction. As technology continues to evolve, the development and refinement of advanced query expansion methods will remain a critical area of focus in the field of semantic search.

The rapid evolution of search technologies has necessitated the development of more sophisticated ranking algorithms that can effectively leverage contextual information. In semantic search, context-aware ranking algorithms stand out as pivotal tools that enhance the relevance and accuracy of search results. These algorithms go beyond traditional keyword matching by incorporating various contextual factors, thereby providing a more nuanced understanding of user queries and delivering results that are better aligned with user intent.

Context-aware ranking algorithms operate on the principle that the meaning and relevance of a query can vary significantly depending on the context in which it is made. This context can include a wide range of factors, such as the user's search history, location, time of day, and even their social interactions. By integrating these diverse contextual cues, these algorithms can rank search results in a manner that is more attuned to the user's specific needs and circumstances.

One of the fundamental aspects of context-aware ranking is the use of personalization. Personalization involves tailoring search results based on the individual preferences and behaviors of the user. For instance, if a user has a history of searching for articles on technology, the ranking algorithm can prioritize tech-related content when the user makes a new query. This personalized approach ensures that the search results are more relevant and engaging for the user, thereby enhancing their overall search experience.

Another critical component of context-aware ranking is the incorporation of temporal information. The relevance of certain search results can change over time, and temporal context allows ranking algorithms to account for these dynamics. For example, a search for "sports news" in the morning might yield different results compared to the same query in the evening, as new events and updates occur throughout the day. By considering the temporal context, ranking algorithms can ensure that the search results are timely and pertinent to the user's current needs.

Geographic context also plays a significant role in context-aware ranking algorithms. The user's location can provide valuable insights into the relevance of certain search results. For example, a query for "weather forecast" should prioritize local weather information based on the user's geographic location. Similarly, a search for "restaurants" should yield different results depending on whether the user is in New York, London, or Tokyo. By leveraging geographic context, ranking algorithms can deliver search results that are more useful and actionable for the user.

Social context is another important factor that context-aware ranking algorithms can utilize. This involves analyzing the user's social interactions and connections to inform the ranking of search results. For instance, if a user frequently engages with content shared by a particular group of friends or follows certain influencers on social media, the ranking algorithm can prioritize search results that are aligned with these social connections. This social context helps create a more personalized and relevant search experience, as the user is more likely to find value in content that resonates with their social circles.

Behavioral patterns are also essential in context-aware ranking algorithms. By analyzing how users interact with search results—such as which links they click on, how much time they spend on a page, and which results they tend to ignore—algorithms can infer the types of content that are most relevant and engaging for the user. For example, if a user consistently clicks on video content rather than text articles, the ranking algorithm can prioritize video results for future queries. This behavior-based approach ensures that the search results are tailored to the user's preferred content format and style.

The integration of multiple contextual factors can lead to even more sophisticated and accurate ranking algorithms. By combining personalization, temporal, geographic, social, and behavioral contexts, these algorithms can achieve a holistic understanding of the user's intent and needs. For instance, a query for "concerts this weekend" made on a Friday evening by a user who frequently attends live music events can be interpreted with a high degree of specificity. The ranking algorithm can prioritize local concert listings happening over the weekend, taking into account the user's location, time of day, and past behavior. This multi-faceted approach ensures that the search results are highly relevant and tailored to the user's immediate context.

Despite the significant advantages of context-aware ranking algorithms, there are also challenges and considerations that need to be addressed. One of the primary concerns is privacy. The use of detailed contextual data requires access to potentially sensitive information, raising issues about data security and user consent. It is crucial for search engines to implement robust privacy measures and provide users with clear information about how their data is being used. Additionally, users should have control over their privacy settings and the ability to opt out of data collection if they choose.

Another challenge is the complexity of accurately interpreting and integrating contextual information. Human language and behavior are inherently nuanced and variable, making it difficult for algorithms to consistently and accurately capture the full context of a query. Ongoing advancements in natural language processing and machine learning are essential to improving the accuracy and effectiveness of context-aware ranking algorithms. These technologies can help algorithms better understand the subtleties of language and context, leading to more precise and relevant search results.

Scalability is also a concern when implementing context-aware ranking algorithms. Processing and analyzing large volumes of contextual data in real-time can be computationally intensive and resource-demanding. Search engines must invest in scalable infrastructure and efficient algorithms to handle the processing requirements of context-aware ranking at scale. This includes optimizing data storage, retrieval, and processing mechanisms to ensure that the algorithms can operate efficiently and effectively.

In summary, context-aware ranking algorithms represent a significant advancement in the field of semantic search. By incorporating a wide range of contextual factors, these algorithms can deliver search results that are more relevant, accurate, and personalized. Personalization, temporal, geographic, social, and behavioral contexts all contribute to a deeper understanding of user queries and a more tailored search experience. However, challenges related to privacy, complexity, and scalability must be carefully managed to fully realize the potential of these algorithms. As technology continues to evolve, context-aware ranking will play an increasingly important role in enhancing the effectiveness and user satisfaction of search systems.

Understanding the user's context is pivotal in enhancing the performance and relevance of search engines. By integrating various aspects of user context, search systems can deliver results that are not just relevant but also personalized to the user's unique situation and preferences. This section delves into the multifaceted nature of user context and explores how different elements can be harnessed to refine search queries and outcomes.

To begin with, one of the primary aspects of user context is the user's previous search behavior. Analyzing prior searches can provide valuable insights into the user's interests and preferences. For instance, if a user consistently searches for topics related to environmental sustainability, the search engine can infer a preference for eco-friendly products or green technology when responding to new queries. This historical data serves as a foundational layer for creating a personalized search experience.

Another critical component of user context is the device being used to perform the search. The type of device—whether it's a smartphone, tablet, or desktop computer—can significantly influence the nature of the search results. For example, a search for "best hiking trails" on a mobile device might prioritize results that include maps and directions, catering to the user's immediate need for navigation. On the other hand, the same search on a desktop might yield more detailed articles and reviews, assuming the user is in the planning stage of their hiking trip. By considering the device context, search engines can tailor results to better suit the user's current needs.

The user's location is another vital element of context that can drastically alter the relevance of search results. Geographic data can help search engines provide localized results that are pertinent to the user's immediate surroundings. For example, a query for "coffee shops" will yield different recommendations depending on whether the user is in San Francisco, London, or Tokyo. This localization not only improves the utility of the search results but also enhances user satisfaction by delivering more relevant options.

Temporal context also plays a significant role in shaping search results. The time at which a query is made can provide important clues about the user's intent. For instance, a search for "dinner recipes" in the late afternoon is likely driven by the user's need to prepare an evening meal, whereas the same query in the morning might be more about meal planning for the week. By incorporating temporal information, search engines can prioritize results that are timely and relevant to the user's current situation.

Social context, derived from the user's interactions on social media and other platforms, is another valuable source of information. By analyzing the user's social connections and activity, search engines can gain insights into their interests and affiliations. For instance, if a user frequently engages with content related to fitness on social media, a query about "workout routines" can be tailored to include results that align with their fitness goals and preferences. This social context allows for a more refined understanding of the user's needs, leading to more relevant and personalized search results.

User interaction data, such as click-through rates and dwell time, also provides important context for refining search queries. By analyzing how users interact with search results, search engines can infer which types of content are most useful and engaging. For example, if a user consistently clicks on video tutorials rather than written guides, a query for "how to knit a scarf" might prioritize video content. These behavioral insights enable search engines to continuously refine their algorithms, ensuring that the results remain relevant and engaging over time.

In addition to these individual elements, the integration of multiple contextual signals can lead to more sophisticated interpretations of user queries. For example, a query for "live music events" made on a Friday evening from a mobile device by a user who frequently attends concerts can be understood with a high degree of specificity. The search engine can infer that the user is looking for real-time information on events happening that night and prioritize results accordingly. This multi-faceted approach to contextual understanding allows for a level of precision that would be unattainable using isolated signals.

However, leveraging user context is not without its challenges. One of the primary concerns is privacy. The use of detailed contextual data requires accessing and processing potentially sensitive information, raising concerns about data security and user consent. Ensuring that users are aware of how their data is being used and providing them with control over their privacy settings is essential in maintaining trust and compliance with regulations.

Another challenge lies in the inherent complexity and variability of human behavior. Contextual signals can help disambiguate queries, but they are not foolproof. Ambiguities and nuances in language can still lead to misinterpretations, necessitating ongoing advancements in natural language processing and machine learning techniques. Moreover, the dynamic nature of context means that search engines must be capable of adapting to changing circumstances in real-time, which requires robust and responsive algorithms.

Despite these challenges, the benefits of incorporating user context in search queries are substantial. By integrating historical, device, geographic, temporal, social, and behavioral contexts, search engines can deliver results that are more accurate, relevant, and personalized. This enhanced relevance not only improves user satisfaction but also increases engagement and retention, providing significant advantages for both users and service providers.

In sum, understanding and leveraging user context is a cornerstone of advanced semantic search systems. By integrating various forms of context, search engines can move beyond simple keyword matching to provide results that truly resonate with the user's intent and circumstances. As technology continues to evolve, the ability to harness user context will become increasingly sophisticated, paving the way for ever more intuitive and effective search experiences.

Semantic query refinement and expansion strategies play a pivotal role in enhancing the retrieval of pertinent information in search systems. These strategies are designed to interpret the underlying meaning of user queries more accurately, thereby improving the overall search experience. By leveraging a variety of sophisticated techniques, search engines can provide results that are more aligned with the user's intent, even when the initial query is vague or ambiguous. This section delves into several advanced methods for refining and expanding queries, demonstrating how they contribute to more effective information retrieval.

One of the core techniques in semantic query refinement is the use of concept-based expansion. This approach involves identifying key concepts inside a query and expanding it to include related terms and ideas. For instance, if a user searches for "renewable energy sources," the search engine might expand the query to include terms such as "solar power," "wind energy," and "hydroelectricity." By focusing on the core concepts and their associations, this method ensures that the search results encompass a broader spectrum of relevant information, thereby increasing the likelihood of satisfying the user's informational needs.

Another effective strategy for query expansion is the use of knowledge graphs. Knowledge graphs are structured representations of information that capture relationships between entities. By leveraging these graphs, search engines can identify and incorporate related entities into the query. For example, a query about "famous physicists" might be expanded to include notable figures such as "Albert Einstein," "Isaac Newton," and "Marie Curie." This graph-based approach not only enriches the query but also provides a more comprehensive set of results by tapping into the interconnected nature of knowledge.

User interaction data also serves as a valuable resource for query refinement. By analyzing patterns in user behavior, such as click-through rates and dwell time, search engines can infer which aspects of a query are most important to users. For instance, if users frequently click on articles about "healthy eating habits" when searching for "nutrition tips," the search engine can prioritize results that focus on dietary habits. This behavior-driven approach allows for dynamic refinement of queries based on real-world user interactions, ensuring that the search results remain relevant and engaging.

Incorporating contextual information is another advanced method for refining queries. Contextual data can include a wide range of factors, such as the user's location, time of day, and current activities. For example, a search for "concert tickets" might yield different results depending on whether the user is currently in New York or Los Angeles. By considering these contextual cues, search engines can tailor the query expansion process to better match the user's immediate situation, thereby enhancing the relevance of the search results.

Temporal dynamics also play a crucial role in query refinement. The relevance of certain terms can fluctuate over time, and search engines must account for these changes to provide timely results. For instance, a query about "election results" during an election period should prioritize recent data, whereas the same query at a different time might focus on historical outcomes. By integrating temporal information into the query expansion process, search engines can ensure that the results are not only relevant but also current,

176

thereby meeting the user's needs more effectively.

Probabilistic models offer another sophisticated approach to query expansion. These models use statistical techniques to estimate the likelihood of various terms being relevant to the initial query. For example, a query about "artificial intelligence" might be expanded to include terms like "machine learning," "neural networks," and "deep learning" based on their probabilistic associations. This statistical approach enables search engines to make informed decisions about which terms to include in the expanded query, thereby enhancing the overall accuracy and relevance of the search results.

Interactive query refinement involves engaging the user in the expansion process. In this approach, the search engine presents a list of suggested terms related to the user's initial query, allowing them to select the most relevant ones. For instance, a query about "gardening tips" might prompt the user to choose between terms like "vegetable gardening," "flower gardening," and "organic gardening." By incorporating user feedback, this method ensures that the expanded query aligns closely with the user's specific interests and needs, thereby improving the search experience.

Domain-specific expansion techniques tailor the query refinement process to the unique characteristics of a particular field. This approach involves creating specialized vocabularies and ontologies that capture the terminology and relationships specific to the domain. For example, in the field of medicine, a query about "heart disease" might be expanded to include terms such as "cardiovascular disease," "coronary artery disease," and "heart attack." By leveraging domain-specific knowledge, this method ensures that the expanded query is highly relevant to the field, thereby improving the precision of the search results.

Another innovative approach is the use of collaborative filtering for query expansion. Collaborative filtering involves analyzing the search behaviors of similar users to identify common patterns and preferences. For instance, if users who search for "travel destinations" often refine their queries to include "beach resorts" or "mountain retreats," the search engine can use this information to automatically expand similar queries for other users. This collaborative approach leverages collective intelligence to enhance the relevance of the search results, providing a more personalized and satisfying search experience.

Finally, hybrid methods combine multiple query expansion techniques to achieve optimal results. By integrating concept-based expansion, knowledge graphs, user interaction data, contextual information, temporal dynamics, probabilistic models, interactive refinement, domain-specific techniques, and collaborative filtering, hybrid methods can leverage the strengths of each approach while mitigating their individual limitations. For example, a hybrid system might use knowledge graphs to identify related entities, probabilistic models to estimate term relevance, and user feedback to refine the final set of expanded terms. This comprehensive approach ensures that the query refinement process is robust, flexible, and highly effective.

To conclude, semantic query refinement and expansion strategies are essential for improving the accuracy and relevance of search results. By leveraging advanced techniques such as concept-based expansion, knowledge graphs, user interaction data, contextual information, temporal dynamics, probabilistic models, interactive refinement, domain-specific techniques, collaborative filtering, and hybrid methods, search engines can achieve a deeper and more nuanced understanding of user queries. These strategies collectively contribute to a more effective and satisfying search experience, ultimately enhancing user satisfaction and engagement. As search technologies continue to evolve, the development and refinement of these advanced query expansion strategies will remain a critical area of focus, driving the future of semantic search.

Real-World Applications And Case Studies In Semantic Search

Real-World Applications of Semantic Search in E-commerce

The digital age has revolutionized the way consumers interact with businesses, and e-commerce has become a pivotal platform for retail and trade. One of the most significant advancements enhancing the e-commerce experience is Semantic Search. This technology goes beyond traditional keyword-based searches by understanding the intent and contextual meaning behind a user's query, providing more accurate and relevant results. In this section, we will explore various real-world applications of Semantic Search inside the e-commerce sector, illustrating how it has transformed both customer experience and business operations.

To begin with, Semantic Search has greatly improved product discovery. Traditional search engines often rely on exact keyword matches, which can lead to irrelevant results if the user's query does not perfectly align with the product descriptions. Semantic Search, however, understands the nuances of language and can interpret synonyms, related concepts, and the overall intent behind a query. For instance, a customer searching for "comfortable office chairs" will not only find products explicitly labeled as such but also those that are described as "ergonomic," "supportive," or "ideal for long hours of sitting." This capability ensures that customers can find what they are looking for more efficiently, enhancing their shopping experience and increasing the likelihood of a purchase.

Another notable application is in personalized recommendations. E-commerce platforms collect vast amounts of data about user behavior, preferences, and purchase history. Semantic Search leverages this data to provide personalized product suggestions that align with individual customer preferences. For example, if a user frequently purchases eco-friendly products, the search engine can prioritize displaying sustainable and environmentally friendly items in search results and recommendations. This personalized approach not only improves customer satisfaction but also drives sales by presenting users with products they are more likely to be interested in.

Customer support in e-commerce has also been significantly enhanced by Semantic Search. Many e-commerce platforms now incorporate chatbots and virtual assistants to handle customer inquiries. These AI-driven tools rely on Semantic Search to understand and respond to customer questions accurately. For instance, if a customer asks, "How do I return a product?" the chatbot can interpret this query's intent and provide a detailed response, including steps for initiating a return, packaging requirements, and shipping instructions. This level of support helps reduce the burden on human customer service representatives, allowing them to focus on more complex issues while ensuring that customers receive prompt and accurate assistance.

Semantic Search also plays a crucial role in inventory management and logistics. E-commerce businesses often deal with vast and diverse inventories, making it challenging to keep track of stock levels, product locations, and supply chain logistics. By utilizing Semantic Search, businesses can streamline these processes. For example, warehouse staff can use semantic queries to quickly locate specific products inside a large inventory, even if the exact product name or code is not known. Similarly, supply chain managers can gain insights into inventory trends and demand patterns, enabling them to make more informed decisions about restocking and distribution.

Furthermore, Semantic Search enhances the user interface and overall usability of e-commerce websites. By understanding natural language queries, e-commerce platforms can offer more intuitive search experiences. Features such as autocomplete suggestions, related search queries, and search filters become more effective when powered by Semantic Search. For instance, as a user begins typing a query, the search engine can predict their intent and offer relevant suggestions, making the search process faster and more user-friendly. This improved search functionality can lead to higher user engagement and satisfaction, ultimately driving more traffic and sales for the e-commerce platform.

In addition to improving the customer-facing aspects of e-commerce, Semantic Search also provides valuable insights for businesses. By analyzing search queries and user interactions, e-commerce companies can gain a deeper understanding of customer preferences, emerging trends, and market demands. This data-driven approach allows businesses to adapt their strategies, optimize their product offerings, and stay ahead of the competition. For example, if an e-commerce platform notices a surge in searches for a particular type of product, they can quickly respond by increasing their inventory of that item or launching targeted marketing campaigns to capitalize on the trend.

Moreover, Semantic Search can enhance the accuracy of product categorization and tagging. Accurate categorization is essential for effective inventory management and ensuring that customers can easily find products. Semantic algorithms can analyze product descriptions, reviews, and other relevant data to automatically assign accurate categories and tags to each item. This automation reduces the manual effort required for categorization and minimizes the risk of errors. Additionally, it ensures that products are consistently and accurately represented across the platform, improving the overall shopping experience for customers.

Lastly, Semantic Search fosters a more inclusive shopping environment. Traditional search engines may struggle to accommodate diverse linguistic and cultural nuances, leading to a less satisfactory experience for non-native speakers or individuals using different dialects. Semantic Search, with its ability to understand context and intent, bridges this gap by providing accurate results regardless of linguistic variations. This inclusivity ensures that e-commerce platforms can cater to a global audience, expanding their reach and customer base.

In summary, Semantic Search has become an indispensable tool in the e-commerce industry, offering a multitude of benefits that enhance both customer experience and business operations. From improving product discovery and personalized recommendations to streamlining inventory management and providing valuable business insights, the applications of Semantic Search are vast and transformative. As e-commerce continues to evolve, the integration of Semantic Search will undoubtedly play a pivotal role in shaping the future of online retail, driving innovation, and ensuring that businesses can meet the ever-changing needs of their customers.

In healthcare, the efficient retrieval of data is not just a convenience but a necessity. The sheer volume and complexity of medical records, research papers, patient histories, and clinical trial data demand a sophisticated approach to search and data management. Semantic Search has emerged as a powerful tool to address these challenges, transforming how healthcare professionals access and utilize critical information. This section delves into the various ways Semantic Search is being leveraged in healthcare data retrieval, highlighting its impact on patient care, medical research, and operational efficiency.

One of the most significant applications of Semantic Search in healthcare is in the retrieval of patient records. Traditional keyword-based search systems often fall short when dealing with the intricacies of medical terminology and the diverse ways in which symptoms, diagnoses, and treatments can be described. Semantic Search, however, can interpret the context and intent behind a query, enabling healthcare providers to find relevant patient information quickly and accurately. For instance, a doctor searching for records related to "chronic obstructive pulmonary disease" (COPD) can retrieve documents that mention "chronic bronchitis" or "emphysema," which are commonly associated with COPD. This capability ensures that healthcare professionals have access to comprehensive patient information, facilitating better diagnosis and treatment plans.

Moreover, Semantic Search enhances the accessibility of medical literature and research papers. The vast amount of published medical research can be overwhelming, and finding relevant studies often requires sifting through numerous articles. Semantic Search algorithms can analyze the content of research papers, understanding the relationships between different concepts and identifying the most pertinent studies based on a user's query. For instance, a researcher investigating the effects of a new drug on diabetes can receive results that include studies on related medications, underlying mechanisms, and patient outcomes. This not only saves time but also ensures that researchers have access to a broad spectrum of relevant information, fostering more informed and innovative medical research.

Clinical decision support systems (CDSS) also benefit significantly from Semantic Search technology. CDSS tools are designed to assist healthcare providers in making evidence-based clinical decisions by providing relevant information at the point of care. By incorporating Semantic Search, these systems can deliver more precise and contextually relevant information. For example, if a physician is treating a patient with a rare genetic disorder, the CDSS can use Semantic Search to pull data from various sources, including medical databases, genetic studies, and clinical guidelines, to offer tailored recommendations. This integration of diverse data sources ensures that healthcare providers have access to the latest and most relevant information, ultimately improving patient outcomes.

In addition to enhancing patient care and medical research, Semantic Search plays a crucial role in operational efficiency inside healthcare institutions. Hospitals and clinics generate vast amounts of data daily, from electronic health records (EHRs) to administrative reports. Efficiently managing and retrieving this data is essential for smooth operations. Semantic Search can streamline these processes by enabling staff to quickly locate necessary documents and information. For instance, hospital administrators can use Semantic Search to find specific policy documents, compliance records, or financial reports, even if the exact terminology used varies. This reduces the time spent on administrative tasks, allowing healthcare professionals to focus more on patient care.

Furthermore, Semantic Search can assist in identifying patterns and trends inside healthcare data, contributing to better public health strategies and resource allocation. By analyzing large datasets, such as patient records, treatment outcomes, and epidemiological studies, Semantic Search can uncover insights that might not be immediately apparent through traditional search methods. For example, public health officials can use Semantic Search to track the spread of infectious diseases, identify hotspots, and allocate resources more effectively. This proactive approach to data analysis can lead to more timely interventions and improved public health outcomes.

The integration of Semantic Search with natural language processing (NLP) further enhances its capabilities in healthcare. NLP allows for the interpretation of unstructured data, such as physician notes, patient narratives, and clinical reports. When combined with Semantic Search, NLP can extract meaningful information from these unstructured sources, providing a more holistic view of patient health. For instance, a healthcare provider can use Semantic Search to analyze a patient's medical history, including handwritten notes and transcriptions, to identify relevant information that might otherwise be overlooked. This comprehensive approach to data retrieval ensures that all aspects of a patient's health are considered in diagnosis and treatment.

Moreover, Semantic Search contributes to the advancement of personalized medicine. Personalized medicine aims to tailor medical treatments to individual patients based on their genetic makeup, lifestyle, and other factors. By leveraging Semantic Search, healthcare providers can access a wealth of information about genetic markers, treatment responses, and patient outcomes. For example, a doctor treating a cancer patient can use Semantic Search to find studies on similar genetic profiles and corresponding treatment plans, enabling them to develop a more targeted and effective treatment strategy. This level of personalization enhances the likelihood of successful outcomes and minimizes adverse effects.

In summary, the application of Semantic Search in healthcare data retrieval is transformative, offering numerous benefits that enhance patient care, medical research, and operational efficiency. By understanding the context and intent behind queries, Semantic Search provides more accurate and relevant results, ensuring that healthcare professionals have access to comprehensive and up-to-date information. As the healthcare industry continues to evolve, the integration of Semantic Search will play a pivotal role in shaping the future of medical data management, driving innovation, and improving health outcomes for patients worldwide.

The legal profession is inherently document-intensive, requiring meticulous analysis and interpretation of vast amounts of text. Legal practitioners, including lawyers, judges, and paralegals, often need to sift through extensive case law, statutes, contracts, and other legal documents to find pertinent information. Traditional keyword-based search methods are frequently inadequate for this task, as they may miss relevant documents that do not contain exact keyword matches or fail to understand the nuanced language used in legal texts. Semantic Search offers a transformative solution by enabling a more sophisticated and context-aware approach to legal document analysis.

One of the primary benefits of Semantic Search in the legal field is its ability to understand the context and intent behind a query. Legal language is complex and often includes specialized terminology, idiomatic expressions, and specific legal doctrines. By leveraging Semantic Search, legal professionals can retrieve documents that are contextually relevant, even if they do not contain the exact search terms used. For instance, a lawyer researching "breach of fiduciary duty" can find relevant case law that discusses "violation of trust" or "failure to act in the best interest," ensuring a comprehensive understanding of the issue at hand.

Semantic Search also enhances the efficiency of legal research. Traditional methods often require extensive manual review of documents, which is time-consuming and prone to human error. Semantic Search algorithms can quickly analyze and categorize large volumes of text, identifying key themes and relevant information. This capability allows legal professionals to focus on the most pertinent documents, saving time and reducing the risk of oversight. For example, when preparing for a trial, a lawyer can use Semantic Search to rapidly identify all relevant case precedents, statutes, and legal opinions, ensuring a well-prepared and robust legal argument.

Moreover, Semantic Search facilitates more effective contract analysis and management. Contracts are fundamental to legal practice, and their thorough review is crucial for identifying potential risks, obligations, and opportunities. Semantic Search can analyze contract language to identify clauses related to specific legal concepts, such as indemnity, confidentiality, or dispute resolution. This automated analysis helps legal teams quickly pinpoint critical sections of a contract, streamlining the review process. Additionally, Semantic Search can compare multiple contracts to identify discrepancies or inconsistencies, aiding in negotiations and ensuring that contract terms are consistent and favorable.

Another significant application of Semantic Search in legal document analysis is in e-discovery. E-discovery involves the identification, collection, and production of electronically stored information (ESI) for legal proceedings. Given the volume of digital data generated today, e-discovery can be a daunting task. Semantic Search can simplify this process by accurately identifying relevant documents based on the context of the search query. For instance, in a litigation case involving intellectual property, Semantic Search can identify emails, memos, and other documents that discuss patent infringement, even if the exact term "patent infringement" is not used. This capability ensures that all relevant information is considered, reducing the risk of missing critical evidence.

Semantic Search also plays a crucial role in legal precedent analysis. Legal precedents are previous court decisions that inform future cases, and understanding their applicability is essential for legal practitioners. Traditional keyword searches may not capture the full scope of relevant precedents, especially when different terminology is used. Semantic Search can analyze the underlying principles and outcomes of past cases, providing a more comprehensive view of relevant precedents. For example, a lawyer working on a case involving "negligence" can find precedents that discuss "duty of care" and "breach of duty," even if those specific terms are not mentioned in the query. This thorough analysis ensures that legal arguments are well-supported by relevant case law.

Furthermore, Semantic Search enhances the accessibility and usability of legal databases. Legal databases contain vast amounts of information, including statutes, regulations, case law, and legal commentary. Navigating these databases can be challenging, particularly for those who are not familiar with legal terminology. Semantic Search improves the user experience by providing intuitive search capabilities that understand natural language queries. For instance, a user can search for "laws related to data privacy" and receive results that include relevant statutes, regulations, and case law, without needing to know the specific legal terms or citations. This accessibility democratizes legal information, making it more readily available to a broader audience.

In addition to improving legal research and document analysis, Semantic Search contributes to knowledge management inside legal organizations. Law firms and legal departments generate and store vast amounts of knowledge, including case files, legal opinions, and internal memos. Efficiently managing and retrieving this knowledge is crucial for maintaining organizational effectiveness. Semantic Search can categorize and index these documents based on their content, making it easier for legal professionals to find and utilize relevant information. For instance, a lawyer looking for internal memos on "client confidentiality" can quickly locate all related documents, ensuring that best practices and institutional knowledge are consistently applied.

Moreover, Semantic Search can assist in the preparation of legal documents. Drafting legal documents, such as briefs, motions, and contracts, requires precise language and adherence to legal standards. Semantic Search can analyze existing documents to provide templates and suggestions, ensuring that new documents are well-structured and legally sound. For example, when drafting a motion to dismiss, a lawyer can use Semantic Search to find and incorporate relevant language from previous motions, ensuring consistency and accuracy. This capability not only improves the quality of legal documents but also streamlines the drafting process.

Finally, Semantic Search supports legal analytics and strategic decision-making. By analyzing large datasets of legal information, Semantic Search can uncover trends and patterns that inform legal strategy. For instance, law firms can use Semantic Search to analyze past case outcomes, identifying factors that contribute to successful litigation. This data-driven approach enables legal professionals to make more informed decisions, improving the likelihood of favorable outcomes for their clients. Additionally, Semantic Search can provide insights into judicial behavior, helping lawyers tailor their arguments to the preferences and tendencies of specific judges.

To conclude, the integration of Semantic Search into legal document analysis offers numerous advantages that enhance the efficiency, accuracy, and accessibility of legal research and practice. By understanding the context and intent behind queries, Semantic

Search provides more relevant and comprehensive results, ensuring that legal professionals have access to the information they need to make informed decisions. As the legal industry continues to evolve, the adoption of Semantic Search will play a pivotal role in shaping the future of legal practice, driving innovation, and improving outcomes for clients and practitioners alike.

In today's fast-paced digital landscape, customer support has evolved into a crucial element for the success of any business. Companies strive to provide swift, accurate, and personalized assistance to their customers to maintain satisfaction and loyalty. Traditional methods of customer support often fall short in meeting these expectations, as they rely heavily on manual processes and keyword-based searches that can lead to inefficiencies and inaccuracies. Semantic Search, with its ability to understand the context and intent behind queries, has emerged as a transformative solution in this domain. This section delves into how Semantic Search enhances customer support, offering practical examples and case studies to illustrate its impact.

One of the primary ways Semantic Search improves customer support is through the enhancement of self-service options. Many businesses offer knowledge bases, FAQs, and help centers where customers can find answers to common questions. However, these resources can be challenging to navigate using traditional keyword searches, as users may not know the exact terms to use. Semantic Search addresses this issue by interpreting the underlying meaning of customer queries and delivering relevant results, even if the search terms do not match exactly. For instance, if a customer types "How can I update my payment info?" into a help center search bar, Semantic Search can return articles related to "changing billing details" or "modifying payment methods," thereby providing a more efficient self-service experience.

Additionally, Semantic Search significantly enhances the capabilities of chatbots and virtual assistants. These AI-driven tools have become increasingly popular in customer support due to their ability to handle a large volume of inquiries simultaneously. Traditional chatbots, however, often struggle with understanding nuanced language and providing accurate responses. By incorporating Semantic Search, chatbots can better comprehend the intent behind customer questions and offer more precise and contextually relevant answers. For example, if a customer asks, "What should I do if my order hasn't arrived?" a chatbot powered by Semantic Search can provide detailed instructions on tracking the order, checking delivery status, and contacting support for further assistance. This level of understanding and responsiveness helps reduce customer frustration and improves overall satisfaction.

Moreover, Semantic Search facilitates more efficient case management for support agents. Customer support teams often handle complex issues that require in-depth investigation and resolution. Traditional systems may require agents to manually sift through extensive documentation and previous case records to find relevant information. Semantic Search streamlines this process by quickly retrieving pertinent documents, case histories, and knowledge base articles based on the context of the inquiry. For instance, if an agent is dealing with a technical issue reported by a customer, Semantic Search can pull up similar cases, troubleshooting guides, and expert recommendations, enabling the agent to resolve the issue more effectively and efficiently.

Another significant advantage of Semantic Search in customer support is its ability to provide personalized assistance. Businesses collect vast amounts of data on customer interactions, preferences, and behaviors. Semantic Search leverages this data to deliver tailored support experiences. For example, if a customer frequently contacts support about issues related to a particular product, the system can prioritize displaying solutions and articles related to that product when the customer initiates a new query. This personalized approach not only enhances the customer experience but also increases the likelihood of issue resolution on the first contact, thereby reducing the need for follow-up interactions.

Furthermore, Semantic Search contributes to proactive customer support by enabling predictive analytics. By analyzing patterns in customer queries and interactions, businesses can identify common issues and address them before they escalate. For instance, if Semantic Search detects a surge in queries related to a specific software bug, the support team can proactively reach out to affected customers with solutions or updates, minimizing disruptions and enhancing customer trust. This proactive approach not only improves customer satisfaction but also helps reduce the overall volume of support requests, allowing the team to focus on more complex issues.

In addition to improving the efficiency and effectiveness of customer support, Semantic Search also provides valuable insights for continuous improvement. By analyzing the content and context of customer inquiries, businesses can identify gaps in their knowledge base, training programs, and product offerings. For example, if Semantic Search reveals that customers frequently ask about a particular feature that is not well-documented, the company can update its resources to address this gap. Similarly, if certain types of issues are consistently reported, the business can investigate and address the root causes, leading to better products and services. This data-driven approach to customer support ensures that businesses can continuously evolve and meet the changing needs of their customers.

Moreover, Semantic Search enhances the collaboration between different support channels. Customers often use multiple channels to seek assistance, including email, phone, live chat, and social media. Semantic Search can integrate data from these various channels to provide a unified view of customer interactions. For instance, if a customer initially contacts support via email and later follows up through live chat, Semantic Search can consolidate these interactions, allowing the support agent to have a complete understanding of the customer's issue and history. This seamless integration ensures that customers receive consistent and informed support, regardless of the channel they use.

Another notable application of Semantic Search in customer support is in sentiment analysis. Understanding customer sentiment is crucial for providing empathetic and effective support. Semantic Search can analyze the language used in customer inquiries to detect sentiments such as frustration, satisfaction, or urgency. For example, if a customer expresses frustration in their query, the system can prioritize the inquiry and route it to a senior support agent for prompt resolution. This sentiment-aware approach ensures that customers feel heard and valued, ultimately leading to higher satisfaction and loyalty.

Finally, Semantic Search supports multilingual customer support, enabling businesses to cater to a global audience. Traditional search systems often struggle with language barriers, leading to inaccurate results for non-native speakers. Semantic Search, with its ability to understand context and intent, can bridge this gap by providing accurate results in multiple languages. For instance, a customer support system powered by Semantic Search can accurately interpret queries in different languages and deliver relevant solutions, ensuring that all customers receive the same high-quality support experience, regardless of their language.

Conclusively, Semantic Search has revolutionized customer support by enhancing self-service options, improving chatbot and virtual assistant capabilities, streamlining case management, providing personalized assistance, enabling proactive support, offering valuable insights, integrating support channels, analyzing sentiment, and supporting multilingual interactions. These advancements ensure that businesses can deliver efficient, accurate, and empathetic support to their customers, ultimately driving satisfaction and loyalty. As customer expectations continue to evolve, the integration of Semantic Search in customer support will play a pivotal role in shaping the future of customer service, enabling businesses to meet and exceed the needs of their customers.

In the ever-evolving landscape of academia, the capacity to efficiently and accurately retrieve information is paramount. As the volume of scholarly publications, research papers, and academic resources continues to grow exponentially, traditional search methods are increasingly inadequate for meeting the demands of researchers, students, and librarians. Semantic Search emerges as a transformative technology, enhancing the ability to discover, access, and utilize academic content by understanding the context and meaning behind search queries.

Academic institutions and libraries serve as the epicenters of knowledge dissemination and research. These institutions house vast repositories of scholarly articles, books, theses, and other academic materials. Traditional keyword-based search systems often struggle to meet the complex needs of academic users, as they may fail to capture the nuanced relationships between concepts and the varied ways in which academic topics can be expressed. Semantic Search, with its ability to interpret the intent and contextual relevance of queries, offers a more sophisticated and effective approach to information retrieval in academic settings.

One of the most significant advantages of Semantic Search in the academic realm is its ability to enhance literature reviews. Conducting a comprehensive literature review is a critical component of academic research, requiring the identification and synthesis of relevant studies and publications. Traditional search methods can be time-consuming and may overlook pertinent literature that does not contain exact keyword matches. Semantic Search addresses this challenge by understanding the conceptual relationships between terms and retrieving documents that are contextually relevant, even if they do not contain the exact search terms. For instance, a researcher investigating the impacts of climate change on agriculture can use Semantic Search to find studies related to environmental stressors on crop yields, adaptive farming practices, and policy implications, thereby ensuring a more thorough and comprehensive literature review.

Moreover, Semantic Search enhances the discoverability of interdisciplinary research. Academic research increasingly spans multiple disciplines, requiring researchers to navigate diverse fields of study. Traditional search methods may struggle to bridge these disciplinary boundaries, leading to fragmented and incomplete search results. Semantic Search, however, can understand and connect concepts across different domains, facilitating the discovery of interdisciplinary research. For example, a scholar exploring the intersection of artificial intelligence and ethics can use Semantic Search to uncover relevant publications in computer science, philosophy, sociology, and law, thus gaining a holistic understanding of the topic. This capability is particularly valuable in fostering innovative and cross-disciplinary research endeavors.

In addition to improving literature reviews and interdisciplinary research, Semantic Search significantly enhances the accessibility of academic libraries. Libraries are repositories of vast amounts of information, including books, journals, archives, and digital resources. Navigating these extensive collections can be challenging, particularly for users who may not be familiar with the specific terminology or classification systems used. Semantic Search offers an intuitive and user-friendly search experience by interpreting natural language queries and providing contextually relevant results. For instance, a student searching for resources on "renewable energy sources" can receive results that include books on solar power, journal articles on wind energy, and reports on biofuels, without needing to know the precise classification terms. This intuitive search capability democratizes access to academic resources, making it easier for users to find the information they need.

Furthermore, Semantic Search supports the curation and management of academic content. Libraries and academic institutions are tasked with organizing and maintaining vast collections of resources, ensuring that they are easily accessible to users. Semantic Search can assist in this endeavor by automatically categorizing and indexing content based on its semantic meaning. For example, a digital repository of research papers can be organized by themes such as "sustainable development," "public health," or "quantum computing," allowing users to browse and discover relevant content more efficiently. This automated categorization not only streamlines content management but also enhances the discoverability of academic resources.

Another notable application of Semantic Search in academia is in the development of personalized research recommendations. Researchers and students often seek tailored suggestions for publications, conferences, and collaborators that align with their specific interests and expertise. Semantic Search can analyze users' previous searches, reading habits, and research profiles to provide personalized recommendations. For instance, a researcher specializing in nanotechnology can receive suggestions for the latest articles, upcoming conferences, and potential collaborators in the field, thereby staying current with the latest developments and expanding their professional network. This personalized approach enhances the research experience and fosters greater engagement with academic content.

Moreover, Semantic Search facilitates the identification of research trends and gaps.

Academic researchers and institutions often seek to understand emerging trends and identify areas that require further investigation. Semantic Search can analyze large datasets of academic publications to uncover patterns, trends, and gaps in the literature. For example, an analysis of publications on renewable energy might reveal emerging trends in solar energy research, identify underexplored areas such as ocean energy, and highlight the need for further studies on the socioeconomic impacts of renewable energy adoption. This data-driven insight enables researchers to make informed decisions about their research directions and priorities, ultimately contributing to the advancement of knowledge.

Additionally, Semantic Search enhances the efficiency of academic publishing. The peer review process is a cornerstone of academic publishing, ensuring the quality and rigor of scholarly work. However, finding suitable reviewers for manuscripts can be a time-consuming and challenging task. Semantic Search can streamline this process by matching manuscripts with potential reviewers based on their expertise and previous publications. For instance, a journal editor seeking reviewers for a paper on machine learning can use Semantic Search to identify researchers with relevant expertise in artificial intelligence, data science, and related areas. This automated matching process not only saves time but also ensures that manuscripts are reviewed by qualified experts, thereby maintaining the integrity of the peer review process.

Furthermore, Semantic Search supports the integration of academic knowledge with educational resources. Academic institutions are increasingly incorporating digital resources and online learning platforms into their educational offerings. Semantic Search can enhance these platforms by providing students and educators with access to relevant academic content that complements their coursework. For example, an online course on environmental science can be enriched with access to the latest research articles, case studies, and datasets related to climate change, biodiversity, and sustainable development. This integration of academic knowledge with educational resources enhances the learning experience and ensures that students have access to current and relevant information.

In summary, Semantic Search offers a transformative solution for academic research and libraries, enhancing the ability to discover, access, and utilize scholarly content. By understanding the context and meaning behind queries, Semantic Search provides more accurate and relevant results, facilitating comprehensive literature reviews, interdisciplinary research, and personalized recommendations. Additionally, Semantic Search supports the efficient management and curation of academic content, the identification of research trends and gaps, and the integration of academic knowledge with educational resources. As the academic landscape continues to evolve, the adoption of Semantic Search will play a pivotal role in shaping the future of research and education, driving innovation, and advancing knowledge across disciplines.

In the digital age, multimedia content such as images, videos, and audio files has proliferated, leading to a surge in the demand for effective search methods. Traditional search systems, which rely heavily on metadata and keyword matching, often fall short in accurately retrieving multimedia content due to their inability to understand the context and intrinsic meaning of the media. Semantic technologies have emerged as a powerful solution to this challenge, offering advanced capabilities for enhancing multimedia search by leveraging contextual understanding and rich metadata representation.

Semantic technologies improve multimedia search by enabling systems to comprehend the content and context of media files more effectively. Unlike traditional search methods that depend on manually assigned tags and descriptions, semantic search utilizes advanced algorithms to analyze and interpret the actual content of multimedia files. For example, in the case of image search, semantic technologies can identify and categorize objects, scenes, and even emotions depicted in the images. This capability allows users to search for images based on their content rather than relying solely on textual metadata. A user searching for images of "sunset over the mountains" can retrieve relevant results even if the images are not explicitly tagged with those keywords, as the system understands the visual elements and context of the query.

Video search also benefits significantly from semantic technologies. Traditional keyword-based search methods often struggle with the vast amount of data contained in videos, as manually tagging every scene or frame is impractical. Semantic search algorithms, however, can analyze video content frame by frame, extracting meaningful information such as objects, actions, and scenes. For instance, a user looking for "soccer goals" can find specific video segments showcasing goals, even if the video metadata does not include detailed descriptions. This level of granularity and accuracy enhances the user experience by providing more relevant and precise search results.

Audio search is another area where semantic technologies offer substantial improvements. Traditional audio search systems rely on metadata such as song titles, artist names, and album information. However, these systems often fall short when users search for audio content based on more abstract criteria, such as mood, genre, or specific lyrics. Semantic search can analyze audio files to identify patterns, rhythms, and even the sentiment conveyed in the music. For example, a user searching for "uplifting instrumental music" can receive results that match the desired mood, even if the audio files are not explicitly labeled as such. This capability allows users to discover new and relevant audio content based on their specific preferences and needs.

The integration of semantic technologies in multimedia search also enhances the discovery of related content. By understanding the context and relationships between different media files, semantic search systems can recommend related images, videos, or audio files that users may find interesting. For instance, a user searching for a documentary about wildlife can receive recommendations for related documentaries, images of the featured animals, and sound recordings of their habitats. This interconnected approach enriches the user experience by providing a more holistic view of the searched topic and encouraging further exploration.

Furthermore, semantic technologies enable more personalized multimedia search experiences. By analyzing user behavior, preferences, and past interactions, semantic search systems can tailor search results to individual users. For example, a user who frequently searches for travel videos can receive personalized recommendations for new travel documentaries, destination guides, and related audio content. This level of personalization enhances user satisfaction by delivering content that aligns with their interests and preferences.

One notable application of semantic technologies in multimedia search is in the field of digital asset management (DAM). Organizations often manage vast collections of multimedia assets, including marketing materials, promotional videos, and product images. Efficiently organizing and retrieving these assets is crucial for maintaining productivity and consistency. Semantic search systems can automatically categorize and tag multimedia files based on their content, making it easier for employees to find and utilize the assets they need. For instance, a marketing team searching for images of a specific product can quickly locate relevant files, even if the images are stored in different formats or locations. This streamlined approach to digital asset management enhances operational efficiency and ensures that multimedia content is leveraged effectively.

In social media, semantic technologies play a pivotal role in enhancing multimedia search and discovery. Social media platforms host an immense amount of user-generated content, including photos, videos, and audio clips. Traditional search methods often struggle to keep up with the dynamic and diverse nature of this content. Semantic search algorithms can analyze and interpret the context of user-generated media, enabling more accurate and relevant search results. For example, a user searching for trending videos on a specific topic can receive results that reflect the current trends and popular content, even if the videos are not explicitly tagged with the search terms. This capability enhances the user experience by providing timely and relevant content in a rapidly changing social media landscape.

Another significant application of semantic technologies in multimedia search is in the entertainment industry. Streaming services, video-on-demand platforms, and music libraries host extensive collections of multimedia content. Providing users with an efficient and intuitive search experience is essential for retaining and engaging audiences. Semantic search systems can analyze multimedia content to deliver more accurate and contextually relevant search results. For instance, a user searching for movies with a specific actor or director can receive comprehensive results that include not only the actor's or director's well-known works but also lesser-known projects and related content. This enriched search experience encourages users to discover new content and enhances their overall satisfaction with the platform.

In the educational sector, semantic technologies enhance the search and discovery of multimedia educational resources. Educational institutions and online learning platforms host a wide range of multimedia content, including instructional videos, lecture recordings, and interactive simulations. Semantic search systems can analyze and categorize these resources based on their educational content and learning objectives. For example, a student searching for tutorials on a specific subject can receive results that include relevant videos, interactive simulations, and supplementary materials, all tailored to their learning needs. This comprehensive approach to educational resource discovery supports more effective and personalized learning experiences.

Moreover, semantic technologies enable the development of advanced multimedia search applications in the healthcare industry. Medical professionals and researchers often need to access multimedia content such as medical images, instructional videos, and audio recordings of patient consultations. Semantic search systems can analyze and interpret the content of these multimedia files, providing more accurate and relevant search results. For instance, a doctor searching for case studies on a specific medical condition can receive results that include relevant medical images, video tutorials, and audio recordings of expert discussions. This capability enhances the accessibility and usability of multimedia content in the healthcare sector, supporting better clinical decision-making and research.

To conclude, semantic technologies offer transformative capabilities for enhancing multimedia search by enabling systems to understand the content and context of media files more effectively. By leveraging advanced algorithms to analyze and interpret multimedia content, semantic search systems provide more accurate and relevant search results, enhance the discovery of related content, and deliver personalized search experiences. The integration of semantic technologies in multimedia search applications across various industries, including digital asset management, social media, entertainment, education, and healthcare, demonstrates the broad and impactful potential of these technologies. As the volume and diversity of multimedia content continue to grow, the adoption of semantic search will play a crucial role in shaping the future of multimedia search and discovery, driving innovation, and improving user experiences across different domains.

In the dynamic and ever-evolving realm of social media, the capacity to effectively monitor and analyze vast quantities of data is crucial for businesses, governments, and organizations. Traditional keyword-based search methods often fall short in this context, as they struggle to capture the nuanced meanings and contexts behind user-generated content. Semantic Search emerges as a powerful tool, offering advanced capabilities for understanding and interpreting social media data. This section delves into the practical applications and benefits of Semantic Search in social media monitoring, illustrating its transformative impact through real-world examples and case studies.

One of the primary advantages of employing Semantic Search in social media monitoring is its ability to discern the intent and context behind social media posts. Unlike conventional search systems that depend on exact keyword matches, Semantic Search algorithms analyze the semantic relationships between words and phrases. This allows for a more accurate interpretation of user-generated content, even when the language used is informal or contains slang. For instance, a company monitoring social media for customer feedback on a new product can leverage Semantic Search to identify relevant posts, even if the users employ colloquial language or emojis. This capability ensures that businesses can capture a comprehensive view of public sentiment and respond effectively to customer concerns and preferences.

Moreover, Semantic Search enhances the detection and analysis of trends and patterns in social media data. By understanding the semantic context of posts, these algorithms can identify emerging topics and trends that might not be immediately apparent through traditional search methods. For example, a fashion brand can use Semantic Search to monitor social media for discussions about upcoming trends, such as sustainable fashion or new seasonal styles. By identifying these trends early, the brand can adapt its marketing strategies and product offerings to align with consumer interests, thereby staying ahead of the competition. This proactive approach to trend analysis is invaluable for businesses seeking to maintain relevance in a rapidly changing market landscape.

In addition to trend detection, Semantic Search plays a crucial role in sentiment analysis inside social media monitoring. Understanding the sentiments expressed in social media posts is essential for gauging public opinion and making informed decisions. Traditional sentiment analysis methods often rely on basic keyword matching, which can lead to inaccuracies, especially when dealing with complex or sarcastic language. Semantic Search algorithms, however, can analyze the context and nuances of language to provide a more accurate assessment of sentiment. For instance, a political campaign can use Semantic Search to monitor social media for public reactions to a candidate's speech. By accurately identifying positive, negative, and neutral sentiments, the campaign can tailor its messaging and strategies to address public concerns and capitalize on positive feedback.

Another significant application of Semantic Search in social media monitoring is in crisis management. During a crisis, timely and accurate information is paramount for effective response and mitigation. Semantic Search enables organizations to quickly identify relevant social media posts and assess the situation in real-time. For example, during a natural disaster, emergency response teams can use Semantic Search to monitor social media for reports of affected areas, requests for help, and updates on the situation. This real-time information allows responders to allocate resources efficiently and provide timely assistance to those in need. Additionally, businesses can use Semantic Search to manage their reputation during a crisis by identifying and addressing negative posts or misinformation promptly.

Semantic Search also enhances the ability to monitor and analyze brand reputation on social media. Maintaining a positive brand image is critical for businesses, and social media plays a significant role in shaping public perception. Traditional methods of reputation monitoring often fall short in capturing the full scope of brand-related discussions, especially when users employ varied language and expressions. Semantic Search algorithms can analyze social media posts to identify mentions of a brand, even when the brand name is not explicitly stated. For instance, a tech company can use Semantic Search to monitor social media for discussions about its latest product launch. By identifying posts that refer to the product in various ways, the company can gain a comprehensive understanding of public perception and address any issues or negative feedback effectively.

Furthermore, Semantic Search facilitates the identification of influencers and key opinion leaders on social media. Influencers play a crucial role in shaping public opinion and driving engagement, making them valuable partners for marketing and outreach efforts. Traditional methods of identifying influencers often rely on follower counts and engagement metrics, which may not fully capture an individual's influence inside a specific context. Semantic Search algorithms can analyze the content and context of social media posts to identify individuals who are influential inside particular topics or communities. For example, a beauty brand can use Semantic Search to identify influencers who are driving conversations about skincare routines. By partnering with these influencers, the brand can reach a targeted audience and amplify its message effectively.

210

In addition to influencer identification, Semantic Search enhances the ability to monitor competitive intelligence on social media. Understanding the activities and strategies of competitors is essential for businesses seeking to maintain a competitive edge. Traditional methods of competitive monitoring often involve manual tracking of competitor posts and activities, which can be time-consuming and incomplete. Semantic Search algorithms can automate this process by analyzing social media posts to identify discussions about competitors and their products. For instance, an automotive company can use Semantic Search to monitor social media for posts about rival brands and new car models. This information allows the company to gain insights into competitor strategies and market trends, enabling it to make informed decisions and stay ahead of the competition.

Moreover, Semantic Search supports the analysis of user-generated content for market research purposes. Social media platforms host a wealth of user-generated content that provides valuable insights into consumer preferences, behaviors, and needs. Traditional market research methods often involve surveys and focus groups, which may not fully capture the diversity of consumer opinions. Semantic Search algorithms can analyze social media posts to identify patterns and trends in consumer discussions. For example, a food and beverage company can use Semantic Search to monitor social media for discussions about dietary preferences and food trends. By understanding the context and nuances of these discussions, the company can develop products and marketing strategies that align with consumer interests and preferences.

Furthermore, Semantic Search enables the monitoring of social media for compliance and regulatory purposes. Organizations operating in regulated industries, such as finance and healthcare, must ensure that their social media activities comply with industry regulations and guidelines. Traditional methods of compliance monitoring often involve manual review of social media posts, which can be labor-intensive and prone to errors. Semantic Search algorithms can automate this process by analyzing social media posts to identify potential compliance issues. For example, a financial institution can use Semantic Search to monitor social media for posts that may violate regulatory guidelines on financial advice. By identifying and addressing these issues promptly, the institution can ensure compliance and mitigate potential risks.

In summary, Semantic Search offers transformative capabilities for social media monitoring, enabling organizations to effectively analyze and interpret vast quantities of user-generated content. By understanding the intent and context behind social media posts, Semantic Search enhances trend detection, sentiment analysis, crisis management, brand reputation monitoring, influencer identification, competitive intelligence, market research, and compliance monitoring. These advanced capabilities ensure that organizations can stay informed, respond effectively to public sentiment, and make data-driven decisions in the dynamic and fast-paced world of social media. As social media continues to evolve, the adoption of Semantic Search will play a crucial role in shaping the future of social media monitoring, driving innovation, and improving user experiences across various domains.

www.ingramcontent.com/pod-product-compliance
Lightning Source LLC
LaVergne TN
LVHW081657050326
832903LV00026B/1799